Dedicated to

For Sonya, Daniel and Joshua

Editor's preface

Here is a brief look at how to take control of your finances, and manage your cash flow with care. You may find this book a useful tool for reviewing your finances, and how to handle money; the amount can be small or large. The same kind of commitment is needed. Be accountable and get your finances under your control.

Times may be hard for you at the moment, with more debt stacking up, but if you follow these simple steps, you could be debt free; this book can teach you how to handle your money with care, and avoid getting into debt which may take years to pay off.

It's worth making every penny work for you; because you have worked hard for your money, now you need to watch your investment grow and increase in value. This book will give you an insight on how to make sure you have money put away finances for a rainy day, because eventually, how you handle your money; will become the key for survival during hard economic times.

How to handle your finances

By

Gerry Legister

Also by Gerry Legister

Horsemen of apocalypse

The best value for a vacation

Poetry Bliss

How to handle your finances

By

Gerry Legister

ISBN 9781456321284

Forward

We don't have to reject the dusty realm of money to be happy, in fact, having money in some ways can help to elevate some of the struggles of our society. And transform poverty into cheerful living, having some money saved up is a bench mark that may eventually lead to you owning greater resources.

Money is the jewel in the crown, the security in ambition the reward of labor, and the pearly gates to riches. Without finance, society would have no modification, and the present civilization would soon mysteriously disappear, so it is important how economical we use our finances, not plundering the wealth of other nations to solve the problems of our own inadequacies, money is not a fantasy reward for virtue, it simple the wages we earn, and how we in turn invest the little that we are privilege to have.

Money can also illuminates the danger of greed in our lives, and sometimes bring people to a premature end. How should finance be handling? Is the love of money the root of all evil?

Contents

Chapter one

Beginning of the End

The global financial crisis that we are all facing may be signaling the biblical prophecy of the beginning of the decline of the American empire, which has been the pioneering bedrock of modern entrepreneurs dream. The value of houses will soon be halved, leaving many families facing negative equity and foreclosure.

There will be less credit available to the economy, and it will be dramatically hard for corporate company to borrow than before the credit crunch started to sink in. This is the worse financial crisis since the ending of the First World War, and it will have far reaching consequences.

We have seen the substantial amount of wealth lost as a result of bad management, downgrading the value of housing property by approximately 30 per cent so far, it will come down more yet, the collapse sends a strong long term message to capital management, ending speculation of profitable revival, to all good intense and purpose, the housing market bubble has burst.

In the 1929 great depression, the cause was down to policy error made by the central bank, allowing the money supply to shrink, however in today's market, Fed is taking a more prompt and aggressive attitude towards salvaging something, by the action to pump liquidity into the system. Will this save us from the apparent wrath of God to come? I am not sure low interest rates, market stimulation; share speculation is the answer to society's problems.

Other economists suggest some ways of revitalizing our position on the global economy, with interesting solution offering the access debt ridden society, to recover the market share values and bring about some kind of stimulation, the market clearly needs leverage to see the shrinking financial sector recover, but banks have to take the lion's share of the blame, because they have undoubtedly, over the past few years acted irresponsibly.

We are in this mess because the banks and lending institution have encouraged excessive behavior with no accountability, everyone wanted to profit and have a life of luxury without paying the real price, the boom of house value has drastically declined, stemming from Fed low policy rates, and many people hold to the idea that the quicker the overprice house falls back to common affordability, then the sooner the market will recover.

Economically this will be the worst US recession in decades, which affects not just subprime mortgage crisis, but is possibly a prime breakdown in the complete financial system that we have come to trust, which has not been regulated and properly, and the eventual outcome will imply greater credit losses, possibly up to $2bn.

While the credit crunch swaps different markets, nominal protection is sitting on top of outstanding stock of paltry $6 trillion bonds. The counterpart will inevitably lead to a systematic breakdown, where hundreds of banks and lending institution with large exposure to real estate will go into liquidation and cease to operate. Federal deposit Insurance Corporation sooner or later will run out of cash, this is the beginning of recession and the end of easy money.

Equity share prices will fall alarmingly 50 per cent relative to their peak, we are not yet feeling the full impact of the global meltdown, but all the global economies are entering the conscious mode of recession, signaling the beginning of the end.

Some good news

Rogue traders in the future will be sentence to prison for fraud and breach of trust, been accountable for other people's money carries a measure of responsibility. While jail sentence may not be good enough for some investors who have lost their lifetime savings, it is still good news that the law has been upheld, the damage may have run into billions, which cannot be easily dismiss, someone in each organization will become the fall guy, possibly the devil's advocate or an evil genius.

In the eyes of many people, rogue traders may be heroes , crafty masters of society, preying on the innocent with speculative arrogance, but in the end justice will prevail, the victims will be exonerated and the offered emerges hapless and broke, the scapegoat of greedy conspiracy penetrating the financial industry.

Banks have frankly betrayed many investors with their failure to understand the importance of family finances and the trust develop between them. Resentment can be suppress, but in the end people always want to hear good news about their accounts. Ridiculous charges is hard to accept in recession or out, a financial incentive is advantageous when it is clearly marked who is likely to benefit, hidden cost should be up front, not unsuspecting bitter pill tone nauseated some time later, give the good news now it will cut the risk of losses and heighten speculation of more revenues.

Good news should involved some kind of saving for everyone, not fluorescent flashes of Wall Street holding the symbol that wipes out the glory days, the flag of prosperity hoisted high, is not for tragic nostalgic reasons , we must all can look up with hope, and dream without our dreams floundering into the blackness of demise. Every person likes to hear that they have won some money even if they do not gamble, or bear to entertain the thought of going into the bookmakers, it is still good news, when interest on investment come out favorably.

So here is some healthy advice, if you want your money to work for you, do not put your eggs all in one basket, be diverse with your money, and invest into different sources of income streams, houses, property, bonds, savings, investment accounts, tax exempt accounts, if there is ever such a thing, as a non paying tax account.

Use your credit cards wisely, get the best use out of your credit card when it is needed, do not go over your limit, a credit card is not for doing crazy Christmas shopping to impress people whose company you cannot stand, and always pay balance off. Beware of putting up your house as collateral for business, be sure you have the ability and income source to pay back a loan if you take one out, if you lend money draw up a contract for repayment.

Take out at least 3 different types of savings account, if you are married, most definitely you need a joint account, to keep things in perspective, but when the arguments starts to come in don't be fooled, you will be rolled out, love does not last forever, be independent and have control of your own money. Set up direct debits; let the banks do the donkey work, you just go along for the ride.

2. **How to tell if a recession is on the way**

Financial Planning should encompass long term savings for the future, especially when approaching the age of 40 plus, obviously the most secure option is investment in a house, but there are many other revenue base option available to everyone if this solution is not possible, try then to seek out other investment and regular savings policy which could be your next best bet.

Bearing in mind that every kind of investment carries a minimum amount of risk which could be taken as a simple accumulating method that can be achieve with regularity, base upon consistency and of course taking some consideration for individuals who are on low income, finding a plan to suit their needs will in the long term be worthwhile, so one sure way out from the retirement disaster is to bypass the suppressing anxiety of current despondency and find the avenue that will cautiously engineer a path to debt free realization, by been consciously driven to resolve financial indifference's and meticulously organize personal finances to enhance the later years.

So depending upon your sex and age, if a person has been working since the age of 21years old and contributing to company pension scheme, by the time they have reached 65 years of age they are still expected to live another 20 years and possible longer, therefore I believe we need sound financial advice on how to prepare ourselves for the twilight years with an education in money management.

The long term solution clearly lies in educating our children and grandchildren with the basic understanding of budgeting, and learning the importance of consistent regular saving to alleviate the consequences of being overly indebted, if individuals start early their savings and investment are unlikely to descend back into the desperate level to which we have plunge today,

But what about the millions who have gone already went without ant financial planning? How can we help them? Quiet simplicity, financial planning could benefit a great deal by helping people with their budgeting and switching their debt to cheaper solution, however, I am not overly convince that people who fall
Into money mismanagement would bother using the financial advice line to get clear of bad debt, even if government made the information absolutely free.

Sadly, if people's instinct is to go around and bury their head in the sand of ignorance, they will not be helping they until someone with extreme truth force them to face up to the harsh reality of life. Into money mismanagement would bother using the financial advice line to get clear of bad debt, even if government made the information absolutely free.

3. The decline in a country's economic growth is a sure sign that recession is on the way, with no reliable source to halt deficit spending, and bring about a responsive market recovery, there are worrying signs and apparent indicators when the stock market performs erratic, negative data starts to validate pessimistic views, indicative of business swing, when manufacturing activity begins to feel the brunt of negative performance.
The 1929 Wall Street crash was followed a period of speculative borrowing on the stock market, currently, we are following the same trend with excess borrowing on property, hedge funds, and private equity, where consumer debt has gone out of proportion, investors are on the lookout for new ventures, because they have found out that they have borrowed far too much, and wasted it on frivolous projects.
You can always tell when Recession is on its way, the signs are obvious if you are in the financial sector, it's a time when the economy experience two consecutive quarters of declining growth. (GDP) And when

borrowing money has become a more difficult task than previous months, the negative change in gross domestic product is the usual measuring leverage to indicate when a recession is here.

There are of course some other pointers that you may be familiar with, to give you a more classified list that will tell you when a recession is on the way. Redundancies and job cut backs, the property market will hit a sever down turn, personal and business enterprises find it hard to acquire operational funding, luxury cut backs, rise in travel fares, due to the cost of oil going up by the barrel, confidence in the stock market decline and shares start to fall in value.

Limited job opportunities will present itself , some industries may inevitable suffer a major regress, to avoid closure they could merge with another company to form a greater alliance, but if that option fails, and the company cannot find a buyer or raised the capital to keep them afloat, then the only alternative remained is for them to go into receivership.

By identifying the signs of recession, industries can be alerted to making provision which may see them through the tough times ahead, knowing the effects of Recession how it will cause business output to fall, gives a company time to plan cut backs, and be more strategically organized in saving some jobs, in recession, there is no getting away from difficulties, job cuts are inevitable, but government could be more helpful in the plight of hardship.

Banks and financial sectors will do their upmost to safeguard their own interest by refusing to lend money for further investment projects, because the risk is too great, and there is no guarantee that recovery will take place soon, financial institutes will continue doing business, while making allowance for big bonus to be paid out to their chief staff members.

In almost every case, recession is preceded by a period of excessive borrowing, where consumers may want to borrow money for the purchase of a new home, or to launch the set up of a new business, but the truth is, will any of the financial institutions have enough courage to lend in such risky environment?

As the recession deepens across Europe, EU member countries are now making a desperate dash for cash, the money supply has definitely fallen from gross access to acute shortage, immediate funding is needed by the banks to sure up the short fall. Even though some government have pledge guarantee to make up a good part of the shortage, and prevented a complete banking collapse, the market trend is still on the decline

Global Insight shows that the record decline in output has heaped further pressure on the European Central Bank to cut interest rates, while indicators seemed to be pointing to an accurate downturn, the coming recession will be a time to play a safer game, by sticking close the budget until conditions are more favorable.

Recession will eventually culminate in a global financial crisis, causing sever traumas for families, with jobs losses, mortgage payments will be default on, and the result could undoubtedly be, more people losing their homes in foreclosure.

Bankruptcy is one of the options that are available to individuals and companies, especially when they cannot pay debts that are owed, it is often considered as an alternative course of action, bankruptcy will free a company from overwhelming debts, and provides the opportunity of making a fresh start subject to restrictions. Although bankruptcy sounds bad it is publicly advertised, it should always be taken into seriously consideration.

Bankruptcy also ensures that assts are divided fairly among creditors, individuals can be made voluntary bankrupt by the debtor themselves, or by creditors to whom money is owed, in a company thy will lose all control of assets, and will unable to obtained credit, the implication places much restrictions on the company making it difficult to trade under any other name, and credit rating will be affected even after years of annulment.

Knowing when a recession is coming gives investors the ammunition they need to sell their shares before they plummet and fall further into bear market. Some investors will have been carefully watching the market, and using momentum investing strategies to move their stock to safer markets.

Clever brokers will diversifying their portfolio investment until recession has bottom out, in order to limit losses, ordinary investors needs to be aware of not having all their investment put into one pot. There are certain economic conditions which allow government to get involved with public corporation, for example, lending sectors providing mortgages, banks, and major car industries, may require some financial assistance.

When recession has taken a deeper hold; the acquisition no doubt will make the government legally responsible for settling most of the outstanding debt. The object of their bailout package will restored some measure of confidence in the property market, but it's not enough to save thousands of job cuts, government needs a more stimulus package to protect the economy from crumpling beyond recognition.

In the final 3 months of 2008 we saw recession deepen to an alarming rate, official figures confirmed output across the 15 member state using the single currency fell 1.5% between October and December. This has been the fastest rate of decline since the euro zone was formed in 1999 and marks the third consecutive quarter of decline.

Liquidity bubble

People took advantage of the liquidity in plentiful supply, at every opportunity that arose the tills were clocking up revenues; the lending institutions threw caution to the wind, and began lending billions for high mark up.

It was the opportunity that investors could not pass up, when the unprecedented flow of cheap money began looking for a home to flood the western economies, we saw trade surpluses being recycled stimulating the search for profit, this brought about the mispricing of greater risk as investors naively imagined large sums of return.

The idea sounded safer than they have proved, with interest rates low and lots of money sloshing around in the financial system, investor sought to capitalize on higher assets returns, by increasing the risk, high demand soon squeezed prices, so very little premium was paid for the high risk which had been taken. Error on the side of caution was misjudged, and greater engagement of hazard perception was applied to systematic risk.

With the interest rates low, people took advantage of the liquidity in plentiful supply, at every opportunity that arose the tills were clocking up revenues, the lending institutions threw caution to the wind, and began lending billions for high mark up to unsuspecting people, who found out later, that they could not afford repayments when the rates began climbing again, sub-prime lending was the most visible sign of the debt binge, investors were unable to capitalize on any worthwhile ventures, and the exaggeration of indiscipline caused the liquidity bubble to burst.

Attributing to the cause of the present crisis, cheap money made the world romance with the idea of a leverage spree, individual's borrowed to further invest in property, second homes, and holiday homes on the continent, spread betting on casino condominium ownership, boats, private jets, and material goods. Investors used cheap debt to invest in higher yielding asset against existing investment.

Bank lending grew large and outstripped customers deposits, and the activities were kept off the balance sheet to make the figures look like everything was alright, but the fire of accountability was igniting, and the blaze catching fast with low confidence adding fuel to the situation, banks started showing up the shortage of credit debt became uncontrollable, the haemorrhaging threaten to bring the economy to a sever standstill.

The result was that sub-prime mortgage borrowers began to default on monthly payment, the market rediscovered the element of risk, but by then the consequences was devastating, in search for yield the liquidity bubble has exploded; we are now living in an age when vast amount of capital has been lost to bad business practices. Fuelling the cycle of bubble and burst when capital investment flooded into the economy, it was later washed away by banking crooks neglecting good business practices and discipline

The money managers soon panic, leaving their responsibility for others to clean up the mess caused by free market system, now tax payers are expected to foot the heavy restaurant bill for the just and the unrighteous, if the state step in the risk and rewards all will belong to the state.

If banks were vigilant, accounting would have brought a greater openness to company accounts, and in fairness turn things around, forcing banks to admit to the market price of securities on their balance sheet, but with no markets for many of these assets, banks had to take a gigantic write off, creating the crisis of spiralling lost, and without enough liquidity confidence began eroding away faster than the blink of an eye.

Many financial advisors, traders, and greedy bankers lost their jobs, but in the ensuing process they will have made millions in short term pay out bonuses for market speculation. Bankers knew what was happening, they also knew what

they were doing was unjust, but they let it continued because the result would favor their pockets in short term result, the finger of blame points widely to many areas of mismanagement, government bailout will only be an attempt to curb greedy bankers pay

3. Bad news

Sickness is a state of mind and body that many people do not have the will power to overcome, being diagnosed with the dreaded critical illness of cancer, is rather a very serious life threatening situation, one in every three of us will one day receive this sad news, when we have reached a certain stage in our lives, and possibility well before we have reached retirement age, it is arguably the biggest threat to healthy living and loss of lives.

In most cases you would expect your health insurance policy to honor the contract and pay out automatically but the new policies are rewriting the modern changes, and are looking deeper into the issues of illness, but rather than paying out, and leave you focusing on getting better, advance medical treatment has made it possible for cancer patients to sometimes make a complete recovery, which as result has made many health insurance policies void.

Insurance policies will only definitely pay out in the absolute certainty of terminal illness conditions, most people are not looking for to take place in their lives, will happen in the shady Grey area of ill health, thinking all is well if the bad news comes from the doctor, but worse news will inevitably follow from the insurers, people will not receive the money they were hoping for if recovery takes place.

Just because a patient has been diagnosed with something that resembles serious complication, when it comes around to talking insurance, paying out is another matter, and not one that is quickly encouraged until all tick boxes are carefully filled in, which means if you have such policies in place, it's worth checking the small prints, and see exactly what the insurance companies will pay out on.

In most instances, private health care will help speed up the process to fund the appropriate medication, stand alone critical illness cover will pay out in a lump sum on the strength of the diagnosis, specifying the condition that the patient is suffering from, 20% of all applications claims fail, because financial advisers have rejected the definition of illness as none life threatening.

The good news is that if a patience recovers from cancer they will live longer, bad news is, if the illness is not consider severe enough, it is unlikely a payout will be made, only critical illness warrant payment, depending on the severity of the case, if customers fail to disclose vital information to the insurers, and the trend is picked up on, claims will be refused.

After making a critical insurance claim, it's the beginning of sorrows and the end of security cover, the only way up is by taking the depressing way down, almost forgotten, most assuredly abandon by society, when you're sick you are no good to anybody, your existence is a burden for others.

4. **Defining Health**

Our world and its environment already has adverse conditions, that many people can identify with, exposure to pollutants through water food and air, the extreme weather conditions, the clinically undesirable HIV infection, irregular palpitation from substances abuse, adverse cardiovascular reactions to over active indulgence, the smog and filth in the cloudy atmosphere, unemployment and homelessness, mental health and the quality of decent lifestyle has steadily eroded into expensive survival kits.

The unidentifiable spirituality related to exposure of the occult, producing the pattern of extreme behavior, mutating disease with adverse effect, which increases the risk of heart disease, stroke and death, are all too common in our world. Modern unhealthy lifestyle means we are no nearer to eternal youth than our predecessors were, in view of our corporation to enlist membership in sports recreation, life still holds no guarantee.

Despite every effective remedy and cost effective diagnostic treatments that we are privilege to have woven into the infrastructure of our modernistic society, our unhealthy habits have targeted high blood pressure levels and the cure for cancer and other colostomy complications are very rarely reached, millions find themselves in this painful category, unable to recover from critical illness even though the price of medication has become affordable in most countries.

The cost of medication is not an issue; rather it's the recovery process which is still playing catch up. Government from time to time speedily rushes through legislation's which please themselves and the national democratic process, on face value, caring very little for citizen's rights, privileges and health, rightly assimilating that national security needs to be more of a higher priority.

By adopting a zero tolerance and taking no chances with the overcast shadows of terrorism, nor should we supporting any activities associated with bringing harm to fellow mankind, or lend encouragement to anything that falls below the standards of our human rights, dissidents should be given a small corner to express their views in a harmless manner, arguably a statement which we mostly are in agreement with.

But we see in society a turning point for the worse behavior in our inner cities, government have omitted the weightier matters of prevention, and have stood by watching root problems in heath deteriorate worse, the medical profession needs more aid to assist in locating cause and cure.

Take blood pressure for instance it is a like bargain within the biggest organ of our body the brain, sending acute messages to the kidneys and other blood supplying areas, moving like a vessels, in unhealthy streams flow from the brain to water different parts of the body with complications.

likewise this is a theory of mine, that high blood pressure may lie within the brain, rather than with problems relating directly to the heart, kidneys or blood vessels, and we need to find new ways of treating the condition. And I am a great believer that we can help ourselves in a perfectly normal way.

Blood pressure is pump around the body by the forceful thrust of the heart, and is measure by two numbers; the first figure is the maximum pressure in the arteries when the heart beats and pushes blood out into the body, the second figure is the minimum pressure in the arteries between beats when the heart relaxed to be filled with blood, the maximum pressure is always listed first, then the minimum pressure a typical normal blood pressure reading may look something like 110/70 elevated maximum and minimum pressure.

High Blood pressure which causes strain on the arteries may result in increase of severe heart attack, possible disease and stroke. What are some of the main causes of high blood pressure? And I want to cover briefly how to avoid the risk factor of heart disease, stroke and kidney failure, and you may ask yourself, what can I do to stabilize elevated blood pressure levels?

well first of all, Some of the most common areas are resulted in family history, your progressing age, smoking and your diet, including alcohol intake, over indulgence of salt and the complete lack of physical exercise, overweight and other medical problems, blood pressure symptoms may go on unnoticed for a long time, until it causes a major blow requiring immediate treatment, it is important therefore and essential that a person gets regular check to detect any change in blood pressure.

Naturally the older a person gets the more prone they become to certain illness, the symptoms of elevated blood pressure may not be noticeable at first, but very severe hypertension symptoms can cause headache, drowsiness and confusion, however, your lifestyle will soon have to change after you have consulted with your doctor, but lifestyle may not be the only change this to be made in order to reduce high blood pressure, you will need medical treatment, and if left untreated it could result in severe complications.

Your health is the most important gift in life so treasure it well; give yourself the best possible chance for recovery. And reduce the risk of blood pressure. Too much alcohol can raise blood pressure levels, even though individuals suffering with hypertension can reduced their risk of a heart attack by having a drink each day, but with alcohol there is a fine line between the defining good health care, and the practical side effects that a person gets.

In reality we should all try to practice prevention before looking for a cure, the warning signs are never too far away from our eyes and ears, there is a risk element in alcohol consumption, and further to that warning, alcohol should never be mixed with medication because it would soon become a total recipe for disaster and could lead to fatal consequences.

But clarification on the subject is a process which needs to be made absolutely clear, that alcohol is not a medicine but can act as a stimulant in limited circumstances, moderate alcohol consumption has in the past prove to actually reduce the risk of heart attack even if a person has had high blood pressure, and some individuals are more healthy than none drinkers. But also remember that drinking to dangerous excess levels carries serious health risks. However sociable you may feel, always be practical and act responsible this will keep your brain still in good working check.

5. Bleeding from the heart

We watch the security of our finance crumble in trading blows, and what was perfectly normal has disappeared, In exchange; we are given the balm of hope as only a temporary measure. But there is a certain part of our heart that will go on forever.

We need divine intervention right now in our world, we lift our hands and bow our knees, in God's presence, we need a favor, to stop the bleeding heart, to stop fear, and mismanagement, the prayer is for God to give us a new hope, right where we are in our inept faltering state, even as we put our hope in each other, our concerns are insurmountable.

The heart of our nation is bleeding. None of the policies seemed to making it right, all ideas have lost its strength in the addiction of daily argument, and poverty and death is a stronger drug crueler than before. As in dreams we hope that one day serenity will follow the heart into a magical place.

We need you lord, in streams of faith resources, love us not as we love you, help us, although we have tempted you; with indiscipline measures we have deprived the fellowship of the Holy Spirit. But In the twilight of this dispensation, the aspect of fear continues to incite our heart to bewilderment.

We watch the security of our finance crumble in trading blows, like building bricks falling one by one, on top of each other, the pile resembles the ashes of sin trampled underfoot, and when hope is almost gone we are left with only a prayer, to forgive us of our trespasses, and create in us a clean heart.

In exchange, we are given the balm of trading as only a temporary measure, but the die is cast and we are on the downward spiral, politicians are just mere mortals not miracle workers, but we stand together in trials and crosses, making mistakes and learning to pray, earning what we deserve, the fruits of ill gotten gain has caught up with the smugglers and overtaken the wreck.

Who are we to blame for the nervous equilibrium state we have gotten ourselves into? Adam and Eve lost the paradise garden of Eden, and there was absolutely no going back, are we are about to lose our world to a defining moment in history? Where prophecy comes based upon the wrath of implemented bio chip.

Even the bible contains messages about the use of our finances for business purpose. /

Revelation 13:17 "**And that no man might buy or sell, save he that had the mark, or the name of the beast, or the number of his name.**"

Deception everywhere has brought the credit system of earth to a standstill, unless there is remarkable intervention, all kingdoms will try to assure depositors that their concerns will be safe, giving a guarantee of returnable bond, but there will be sleepless nights from now on, and the anxiety over finance will grow deeper, followed by the numbing sensation of the pale hose bringing up the rear.

We humans, on earth, stands at the threshold of losing credibility, and all the privilege that citizens had taken for granted, but where sin abound, grace goes a step further, and the outreached hand of tender mercy abounds where sin has left its marked, someone had to pay for the respect of human life so the message can be more relevant today, we were given the key to heaven, now we have lost everything and still bleeding from the heart.

Slain to cover our shame, I am only breathing because I am bleeding like you, bleeding every day, trying to make things right, I am like the man whose blood flowed from the ripped wound, hung limpidly on the criminals cross, with his head bow in deep contrition; he was wounded for our transgression, and bruised for our iniquities, and he likewise died from a broken heart.

6. **Stocks to avoid**

Smart investors will know the financial pitfalls to avoid, and are keen to capitalize on the optimism of prudent assurance, where their money can be safer harness to produce inevitable profit, so that they can avoid right across the board, bad economic investment. In the financial sector, there will always be winners and losers, but if you can avoid sinking into the bottomless pit, by adopting a clever way of diversifying stock, you will find yourself in a better position to make incredible gains.

Domestic initiatives have dominated the current financial crisis, with many people believing that the worst is yet still to come, it's only natural to try and figure out which stock is best to avoid, some stock that looks good, would be well advise to stay away from, but separating the good from the bad, is not easy without some kind of guideline, because in reality, all stock offers the chance to make some gain by taking a little risk.

The best way to avoid stock loses is not to put all your money into one retirement plan, because prices go up and down, diversifying your stock holdings helps to alleviate that problem, and you can avoid stock loses , if something dramatically goes wrong with that particular industry that you have invested heavily in.

A smart investor who is financially conscious about stock, should avoid careless measures by showing a degree of intelligent correlation, most companies will be affected by economic changes, but the degree of imbalances that may affect one company, the negatives and forecast may not necessary affect another.

Owning different stocks that are none correlated, which simply means, that they are not of the same industry; manufacturing or supplying, diversity is a mixed bag, having small growth and cap valued investment percentages, will enable you to avoid the financial pitfalls.

Some stock will perform well in 2009, while others will feel the effect of the credit crunch, and negative equity will create problems, positive adjustment will be needed to stem the tide of companies bleeding cash, some industry have a history of staggering losses, namely in the home entertainment sector, and

I can see Blockbuster, Inc. (BBI) not doing well. Computer competition gives blockbuster hardly any future, because there are cheaper alternative ways of acquiring movies, online streaming with instant access is the modern convincing way of renting entertainment.
Another dubious one to watch out for during 2009 is Vonage Holdings Corp. (VG) The voice
Of broadband protocol providing service to small business and residential customers. They will be battling against the tide, going against other notable internet giants with greater resources and funding. Cash and bonds are of course good long term investment, Gold has come back in a big opinion way, but as you know, the heartbeat of the market is investment trust, characterize by the different companies and how they managed your money, steer well clear of semiconductor stocks, with low collateral and greater debt obligation, stock like derivatives junkies, internet software (ISO), subprime failures, car manufacturing industry, and exposure to risky business that will set your nerves back to the dangers of stressful levels.

The leveraged by which success is measured, can be the difference between the bank balance and collateral deterioration, or loses and gain, stocks are always under attack by banks who wants to exploit rock bottom prices, and the gamble is a risk, generating massive profits for banks and brokers alike.
For homebuilders the worse is still yet to come and the structure of once stable investment is now quickly collapsing, eroding away faster than the careful orchestrated measures; they once took in building a magnet empire. Visionary reality Companies that go around giving away things free will eventually plunge into decline through the avenue of misappropriation. While the recession is taking severe effect on a number of industries, it may be wise to consider a list

of stock to avoid, mainly sideway traders, and undercapitalize companies that will shrink and jettison into damage limitation. The forecast for the tough economic times ahead, is for investors to look at stock handing profit over for a small investment regardless of how bad stock trading gets.

7. **How to profit from a recession**

There are a number of adventurous people who specialize in making a profit from the misfortunes of others. They do this by taking advantage of circumstances around them, and making good use of assessed information about financial investing. In a tenacious show of positive persistence, they will make an expedient path to success seem normal, by strategically planning how to come out on top during periods of gross domestic downturn.

Those in the banking sector can profit from the awards of large bonuses because they could have a more stable resistance to a difficult climate. With the analyses of figures at their disposal, and the generous acquisition of constant steady cash coming onto the balance sheet, they may find themselves in a better position to exercise caution more than industrial manufactures of goods.

To address the equilibrium for ordinary investors, the opportunity may lend credence to the state in which they find themselves, budgeting and careful planning is the way forward, however, rarely do businesses that are streaming a head, make provision and safeguard investment from possible catastrophe, when business seemed to be going good, why should precaution be taken when another million is just as easily acquired? Perhaps that is exactly the kind of negative thinking that has gotten so some many stagnant companies in financial difficulties; they were negligent in planning for the foreseeable future and certainly unprepared for recession, many of the problems that industries have experience, no doubt, have been self inflicted, starting out with greed, and ending up with embarrassment.

To make profit from a recession, people can invest in businesses that have a well documented diverse portfolio, outlining medium and long term aims and objectives, not just the goals that are immediate, but the ones that could be the catalyst to greater expansion, undergirded with heavy financial backing, where share holders can also get a slice of the profit, and all accountability are in place to alleviate and minimize the risk element.
Dynamic leadership is needed to spearhead the innovations, but not forgetting common sense. Space is currently crowded with all sorts of useless pieces of satellite junk; common sense tells the scientist to stop sending more things into orbit, because inevitably one day they will crash into each other. Recession is a crash, bringing manufactures down to their knees, and the only people who profit, are the ones who have design a way to survive

In recession, assets dwindles, budgets are always squeezed, by rising welfare spending and falling revenues, people lose their jobs, houses are repossessed, and banks don't hesitate long before they pull the plug on those who default on mortgage payments. You can make a profit in a recession, by taking advantage of the strong barging position in which buyers have found themselves.
Recession can encouraged buyers to look around for bargain properties, and take advantage of the steep fall in house prices, knowing that recovery could be a long time in coming, some people are quiet desperate to sell their house, due to job losses, cut backs, the lack of finance, relationship difficulties, marital breakdown, new ventures, emigrating to a different country to live and join other expatriates, upgrading for better condition, or down grading to suit circumstances.

For whatever the reasons realtors are selling, sentimental expression has no lasting interest in a declining atmosphere, circumstances alter cases, and wherever the possibility present itself, or show favorably leverage of making a profit in recession, the opportunity should not go begging, but act upon swiftly. Recession can be a national temporary setback, or a global consumption, being efficient in planning, will not only reduces your spending, but also puts a person in the commanding ascendancy.

Recession makes all kinds of demands on people, from all different walks of life, but industries feel the ricochet more acutely, by taking steps to make workers redundant, instigating cut back on pay rises, and making changes cost effective, some companies have place themselves in precarious circumstances shouldering insurmountable negative equity, while others are slightly better in their approach thinking. Clever thinkers will combine stability and investment for the future, by developing their technology to generate passive income, and with optional measures ratified, they will make considerable effort to merge with sister companies in forming a stronger alliance for survival, until recession is bottom out, the bedrock of durability in times of hardship, is for investors have plenty capital at their disposal to buy low and eventually sell high.

How to invest during a recession

As interest rates continue to fluctuate and create a vacuum of negativity, with lenders and borrowers experiencing the sharp end of the credit crisis, causing more industries to feel the uneasiness of a sluggish economy, the last thing that is on a person's mind is investing. Many individuals are more concerned with finding the avenues of survival, rather than risking another cent on the possibilities in a future of uncertainty.

During the climate of recession, people spend less money, reducing household expenditures, contributing to the fall in demand for goods, the rippling effects continue with employers lay off employees whose service are no longer required, driving down earnings and the fall of share prices. Although there are no obvious signs of indication, individuals may well is showing the symptoms of a nervous disposition brought on by the credit crunch.
But Shares bought when they are low can later rise in greater value, recession can offer the greatest investment opportunities, if you are smart enough to take advantage of the situation, you will emerged much wealthier after the initial decline has dissipated. Bear market is a slow economy; every step taken should be with care, but not with fear.
To put negative assumption in context, some people are unable to undertake portfolio reviews, because they are simply not up to the challenging task of speculation, nor do they embrace the appetite of knowledge for investing during a recession, having read so much into how millions have been wipe of the stock market, with shares plummeting further down each day, and many well establish businesses closing down faster than we can count.

Recession is not a bad time to invest, on the contrary, I expect in recession a broader role is employed, for investors to get a premium return on their investment, good diversified venture capitalists, who invest large sums of other people's money, can take some satisfaction in pointing out information with innovation drives, the way to succeed is to get into the hustle of the market, and be a successful entrepreneur, weathering all economic storms.
When making a strategic investment during a recession, the steps that are immediately taken, could very well yield greater dividends from the opportunities which present themselves, as federal

funds becomes available in a stimulus package to bolster faltering banks and corporate industries.

During The years of shrinkage, when stock declined, some investors realized there was a bargain to be had, and took advantage of the situation, although in retrospect, cool nerves was kept, the ready availability of cash was something that the recession of 1929 had lacked, but government bailouts has given back some impetus to the present market trend, and buoyancy will not be long in coming.

Negativity may not always be stuck in a pedestrian stream, swimming to avoid been drown in the fiscal crisis of a worsening financial economy, when considering that the great depression lasted from 1929 to 1944, there was still many start up programs, entrepreneurs driven by the condition to find solutions, from start to finish, they ventured into capitalism and operated companies successfully, until the recession eventually bottom out 43 months later.

The bear market in recession, commands investors to apply a different strategy, to get the best result from their investment portfolio, by first, taking into account all risk elements before any attempts are made to diversify. Setting up a medium and long term reserve fund, is important to safeguard against job losses and illness, make financial planning with emergency funds to equal out living expenditures, look at your portfolio and see where could be leading to a demise or financial collapse, this could be as a result of fear or the lack of money.

Many companies facing the possibility of closure, were not resourceful in undertaking security measures, in anticipation of job losses and dwindling contracts, if they had done their homework, and saw that more cash was needed to undergird investment, clearly they would still have been in business today, much of the negativity that is spreading pessimism in the atmosphere has been the result of negligent and reckless spending.

Although erring on the side of caution, some investors have become too absorb in the negative mode of consciousness, lending support to a further deteriorating situation, which is developing into a global financial crisis, causing ripples to be felt by some of the world's largest economy. They would be of greater value to others and themselves, if they were to be more optimistic, and plan their strategy for limiting capital losses and making good out of the saturated imbalances.

Japan's gross domestic product, or the total value of the nation's goods and services, has dropped alarmingly at an annual pace of 12.7% in the October to December period. The decline has now contracted for three straight quarters, and is set to intensify. Europe and America are still great places to make money from, even with the decline averaging below 4%. Car manufactures and the housing market seemed to be the areas hardest hit.

With a further decline in job opportunities, those with large mortgages have found monthly payments harder to sustain, hardship in repayment has double, especially those who are sub-prime borrowers (typically paying back loans at a higher rate than standard variable deals). Investment has dried up in some sectors, and the effects are painful for some individuals who have adverse credit history, but momentum investing uses strategies to endure rollercoaster slumps.

In recession, some public companies are nationalized, government step in with a big wad of cash to bolster the situation, and of course they will take the lion's share of responsibility, shares will continue to moved from neutral ground to unchartered territory, same as it would do in normal circumstances, the problem recession create is mainly for the economy, but still offer the chance to make some serious profit, by knowing how the market behave and investing sensible.

Chapter two

7. Getting a credit card with bad credit

We are quickly progressing to a cashless system of purchases. Most people now do not carry large sums of money with them when they go shopping, however, they do have other available means by which to purchase luxury necessities, airline tickets and consumer goods, credit in broad terms simple means cash when you need the resource, but how many credit cards does an individual need, will largely depend upon the level of credit they want and can afford to utilize.

For property developers they may need eight or nine, credit cards, but other major business directors and financial investors may need substantially more, but ordinary individuals and small businesses can get by with one or two conveniently suited credit cards.

Every day the popular on-line buying with major credit cards at low per cent interest and other new payment methods are becoming a part of the western way of life. At present it is possible to pay almost any domestic bill online, even set up direct debits and automatic monthly payments where the account holder need not even raise a finger. While obviously this is not yet fraud proof, the convenience often outweighs any risks that are present.

Credit cards was first pioneered for the select few who had the means by which to pay back, but now they are becoming widely accepted for those with less than one hundred percent credit rating, The question remains to be answer, and one that many people are asking in the developing world, how can a person with bad credit be a part of these new beneficial systems? What must they do to repair their credit rating? This includes taking their circumstances in consideration.

Today's envious Credit cards with low APR are for the most part unavailable to consumers that have bad credit, and poor credit rating.

With the global world moving into a recession of poor credit, on a whole, the opportunity is becoming apparent, that more financial institutions are making their products widely available for this new growing market. Creating an accessible payback solution. Granting bad creditors the opportunity to repair their credit, the pilot schemes are becoming more common and the availability is quickly spreading.
More people should have the chance to have a credit card if they want one.
This includes taking their circumstances in consideration. Giving individuals a chance with little or no history, also those that may have had problems in the past. Extending to people with lower than average income.
These bad credit cards can be a decisive advantage to consumers with a poor credit history, but if managed badly can do more harm than good. While some people have bad credit as a result of unemployment or illness, most consumers simply manage their finances badly. Bad credit cards handled poorly will keep a credit rating low, or make it worse.

Bad credit cards can be used for good reason with the ever increasing higher rate of rising interest; bad credit cards can be positively used in the following ways to increase a consumer's poor credit rating:

Essential monthly Use is necessary, so for argument sake, use your credit card to Make at least two purchase each month on selected items, when your statement arrive, pay the balance off entirely, avoiding the charges, this method is the best way to use bad credit cards, the result is progressively beneficial, your payment offers a consistent flow of credit reporting on your account. This favorable accountability is the measure of consistency that your creditors are looking for in a good customer.

However, by keeping a small balance you will give the credit company the opportunity to increase your balance, many budgeting financial expert will of course tell you the plain advantage, that you should to pay off your credit card balances as fast as and as quickly as possible, Credit companies like customers to carry a balance for obvious reasons, and the only real benefit is so they may increase your balance because of this. You'd be amaze how many problems can be solved by having a credit card, so the risk element is, DO NOT carry a balance that will cause you to get behind in payments due to high APR.

there is a minimum amount of payment that you can make each month, but this benefits the credit card company, rather than improving your status, The more debt incurred on credit cards, the less credit worthy you are likely to be. A safe point of how to measure your credit, and stay one step ahead of high charges, is to keep a little less than half of your available credit limit open across all your credit accounts.

And it's not unusual for creditors to sell customer accounts to other competing credit companies as good credit worthiness exchanges. If it has happen to you, be assured that you are not the only one; it's a common practice in the industry, and one that is resourcefully revenue clever, because as a customer becomes more credit worthy, over a period of time, they also become more valuable to many other creditors. Building the business up to make a greater profit, some credit companies, especially favorable to bad creditors, will help customers build their credit back up, and then sell them to another company. This can be a good change for the customer and may well lead to their new account having a have better APR.

unfortunately there is a down side for individuals with very bad credit rating, this comes as a result of possibly several negative circumstances, so with little or no hope, cash for the moment is one of their only monetary means of paying for goods obtained, where a credit cards is specifically required, but due to the vast amount of repossessions and foreclosure, many people have fallen into an unwanted position of negative equity, unable to make payments on time, also due to lots of regular employment or severe illness, It is possible to have credit that is so bad that even those selected companies that specialize in issuing bad credit cards won't issue individuals a credit card. Once this point is reached,
It is quite possibly that through bankruptcy or administrative liquidation bringing company closure and lots of income, realistically, debit cards and prepaid credit cards will become the only options left. Debit cards work the same as credit cards when making a purchase for the most part, and they can't get you into any further credit problems. If no funds are not in the account, prepaid cards work exactly like a credit card; however money must be deposited into the prepaid credit card account before they can be used.
With all of these new and interesting options open to consumers, there something out there to meet everyone's budget, bad credit cards made widely available will allow just about every individual to take part in our modern economy. With careful budgeting

and money management consistent repayment effort over a continuous period of time, even the worst person with a bad credit history can be repaired. Typical example of what comes with a bad credit card that can be use for good reason.

18. **A guide to credit repair**

The best way to repair your credit rating is to maintain one credit card and make regular payments on all loans and other financial obligations in compliance with your monthly budget, cut back on non essentials and make regular contribution to clear outstanding debts, one of the most important strategic move that you can make is to plan your monthly budget and follow it persistently spreading the cost of household items evenly, be strict with yourself with regards to social activities, treat your credit repair as you would do any other project management by combing your debts to integrated management resolved, where all debts however large or small are taken into a pool of repayment.

But essential sacrifices will be needed in order to maintain a high level of dominance, where feelings of guilt and sympathy are calmly put aside and the emphases is place upon the focus of salvage, it's not unusual for creditors to sell customer accounts to other competing credit companies as good credit worthiness exchanges. If it has happen to you, be assured that you are not the only one; it's a common practice in the industry, and one that is resourcefully revenue clever, because as a customer becomes more credit worthy, over a period of time, they also become more valuable to many other creditors. Building the business up to make a greater profit, some credit companies, especially favorable to bad creditors, will help customers build their credit back up, and then sell them to another company. This can be a good change for the customer and may well lead to their new account having a have better APR.

unfortunately there is a down side for individuals with very bad credit rating, this comes as a result of possibly several negative circumstances, so with little or no hope, cash for the moment is one of their only monetary means of paying for goods obtained, where a credit cards is specifically required, but due to the vast amount of repossessions and foreclosure, many people have fallen into an unwanted position of negative equity, unable to make payments on time, also due to lots of regular employment or severe illness, It is possible to have credit that is so bad that even those selected companies that specialize in issuing bad credit cards won't issue individuals a credit card. Once this point is reached.
It is quite possibly that through bankruptcy or administrative liquidation bringing company closure and lots of income, realistically, debit cards and prepaid credit cards
Will become the only options left. Debit cards work the same as credit cards when making a purchase for the most part, and they can't get you into any further credit problems. If no funds are not in the account, prepaid cards work exactly like a credit card; however money must be deposited into the prepaid credit card account before they can be used.

With all of these new and innovated interesting options open to consumers, there is something out there on the market to meet everyone's budget, damaged credit can be repaired with consistent repayment on bad credit cards which has been made widely available for everyone and will allow just about every individual to take part in our modern economy. Bad credit is no longer an insurmountable brick wall, but anyone with adverse details against information against their name can have their credit file repaired, with careful budgeting and money management consistent repayment effort over a continuous period of time, even the worst unfortunate person with a bad credit history can look forward to credit Independence.

Typical example of what comes with a bad credit card which can assist in making lower purchase interest rates a realistic possibility, always used credit cards wisely and cover your balance by paying more than your monthly minimum payment on time, bad cards are beneficial to individuals if they are use for good reason.

- No annual fee
- Up to 56 days interest free on purchases
- Free additional card holder
- Free fraud monitoring - we'll warn you of any suspicious activity on your account
- Chip & PIN technology for added security whenever you use your card
- Visa is widely accepted in the UK and abroad
- Convenient for paying on-line and over the phone
- typical 39.9% APR

Interest rate on borrowing

Barrowing very large amounts of money on your credit card is not advisable, in the long run it will prove more expensive, and while new cars are rolling off the run way into the glassy court yards of new showrooms, not as many people are buying new vehicles, because we are currently in a savers market, where credit on luxuries items are squeezed, the federal reserve, and primary have their work cut out, to keep inflation from becoming a runaway express train.

The cost of loan borrowing has driven down traditional lenders, despite the warning of gloomy outlook and the effects it is causing, if you really have to borrow money it's worth looking at the interest rates you will be paying back, lower interest rates reduces the total amount of credit.

Interest rates is the income derived from banking, which go up and down because more people want money to borrow, and lenders who are willing to fund loans hike up their interest rates, however, if the demand for credit reduces, there will also be reduction on interest rates of ordinary borrowing, but the distinction must be made on the different products, giving buyers the option of flexible purchasing at lower interest rates, especially on new mortgage for first time buyers.

After passing the borrowing criteria, and assessing the risk of how the debt will be paid, lending industry will charge interest rate on the total amount of loan funded, borrowing large amounts over short term obviously will attract access liquidity interest, along with the risk elements, the clever thinking is to get an agreement on the lowest interest rate that you can.

Interest rates can be fixed on variable products, and mortgage payments are calculated by affordability, but mortgage interest rates in particular may fluctuate rapidly with little or no warning, especially on interest only and adjustable rates, which are subject to changes at any time, the mortgage interest rate on an average 30-year fixed rate mortgage is 6.50% from various lending sources.

the best standard interest rates includes insurance cover, at 6.71% APR secure borrowing on your home, the interest rate will fall back little lower, but in the current financial climate, it's worth avoiding secure loans where your home is at risk and can be taken as collateral.

By limiting the risk on your house, unsecured loans makes it impossible for companies to take away your home, if you default on payment, you can achieve this by going to private lenders who will consider your application, and your credit rating will be made available to lenders who will be liable for a portion of the loan.

Lenders criteria is tight at moment, with the gloomy atmosphere feeding on the economy, central financial mussels, are trying to open the purse wider to encourage investment, even the primary discount rate to other banks, are trimmed in a high spin move to show relative upbeat effort in commitment, by cutting their interest rate from 5% down to 4.25%, so when looking for unsecure loan, it makes more sense to look for financing with lower competitive rates. The fall of house prices has resulted in lenders tightening up on mortgages to protect losses.

Whenever the economy is booming there is a greater demand for working credit, resulting with interest rates going up, But in real financial terms, when the economy has slowed down, it presents less demand for credit, the atmosphere will causes lenders to reduce their interest rates, and depending on the overall state of the economy, encouragement is to stimulate consumer spending, by cutting interest rates.

When interest rates are cut, life's luxuries start to creep into Peoples mind, because they will have more surplus money to spend on cars, boats, fantasy and dream holidays, consequently, they will pay less on their mortgages with the option to borrow more money.

The major reason why interest rates go up and down is largely due to the cost of inflation, and the correlating with price increase on goods and service charges, higher inflation is closely associated with our expanding economy, when the federal reserve cut rates it usually affects the bank interest rates, which also reduces customers rates for borrowing.

This measure only affect the average person with a short term loan, but the cuts puts a limit on the interest you will receive on CD deposits. In order to keep inflation under control the action is unavoidable, because our economy is among the World's largest, with greater potential to expand.

Therefore, the Federal Reserve has put a rescue plan in process, by cutting interest rates from 4.5% to 4.25%. For the third time in a row, the changes are running concurrently, however, when there is a rise in interest rates, it will cost borrowers a lot more to make their mortgage payments.

Bank managers

Should we absolve those who go out of the black and into the red? Carrying the burden for them, and afterward apply the rules of the sabbatical year to release bad debt? As emotions run high and pressure mounts, no one begrudges a person with large credit cards balance, the crunch simply means, there will be a lot less money available to borrow, and discarded bankers can grieved like the bereaved.

Financial debt is the new fact which is reflecting the condition of society in which we live, showing the markets worst reaction and the kneeling disparity of government officials, thrashing out rescue package which is not as easy as it may sound; to implement security guidelines requires consistency in regulations. Common sense is not something that can be bought with large salaries it is already within our grasp.

Bankers have live on lottery size salaries and bonuses, fueled by excitement and incredible amount of luxuries, fullness of bread and a lifestyle not in sympathy with the less fortunate, now they are dejected and suffering from drunken irritability's with the sour unmoved pain of grief loitering near their porches and penthouses, seeking a quick divorce from debt which so far has eluded them.

The bygone financial bill would allow the US treasury to purchased troubled mortgage assets from financial institution, so that the banks can resume lending as quickly as possible, the proposed bill would have let the US government to go ahead with $700bn rescue plan, the house of representative and senate voted against the bail-out. No doubt the overwhelming contentious bill has a sinful price tag, and the debt must be paid.

After the unregulated fashionable hallucination of festive luxury, which at the time seemed quiet harmless, we are now entering into a period of time where the trespass of sin has been called to account in tearful confession, financial behavior like firing loose cannon, has resulted in hopeless indebtedness, by the now quivering insomniacs fat cats who were lying, cheating, stealing and rough riding between banks.

Jesus turned the money changers out of the temple with a whip and a stern warning that the wages of sin was debt; upon which generation has shambolic binge themselves, and the severe effects are coming out in testimonials by debtors harmful behavior, contributing to more agony, where the lives of family and loves ones have been completely destroyed by the lack of admonition.

Since we are all now in a learning classroom, its perhaps not too late to impose penance upon those who have spent the jewel in the crown, in a life of wastefulness, However, if we connect the beginning of the crisis we will get an equation near the beginning of the end of the American empire. Financial debt is not only a spiritual metaphor of sin; it is the relevance of sinful condition the sovereignty has found itself in.

The banking system has collapse as a result of not having proper regulations in place, with the whole banking institution falling apart, leaving a vacuum of heavy debt which in a bible sense is a form of naive slavery, how do we worked this one out? Sermonizing is not the answer, the nicely put together compatible package bail-out has failed, the impossibility has become possible, and the notion that debt is now intrinsically connected to our every move.

At last, people are sitting up and thinking about the extreme behavior Jesus took with the money changers, impolitely driving them out of the temple, and reinstate law and order, this must have been a very difficult course of action for the master to have taken, but it was the only sensible avenue with a lesson to be learned.

Now after the horse has bolted, everyone is encouraged to follow the cautious example by a strict curbing of overspending, which should have been done in the first place. And soon the horror and burden of been in debt will claimed lives, the joys we once shared will have to be paid for, the only virtuous honor remains, is for those bank robbers and money changers, be to simply burn their insurmountable accounts, and turn their lives over to Jesus for forgiveness.

Greedy covetous traders in suits on Wall street, have lined their own pockets, forgetting about Main street, and have hidden the gold in the ground, if somehow we were to grant absolution of debt the guilty parties would walk free, and despised the deadbeat, possibly going on to rake up more financial impropriety elsewhere. Ultimately, Achan in the book of Joshua repaid somehow for the stolen debt.

There is a familiar revival ring about the present crisis, going in and out of fashion like any other spiritual related sins, adultery, theft, drunkenness, murder, rape, prostitution and unbelief, are all tempting areas which we are called to take the utmost care lest we venture into potential disaster, trespassing means overstepping into another person's property, presumptuously removing the old landmark and breaking the carefully defined boundaries.

Debts should have been paid back in a matter of weeks or months, instead we find ourselves been allowed to borrow up to six times our annual salary with guidelines as soft as milk and honey, in the lord's prayer there is a line which contained, "forgive us of our debt as we forgive those who trespass against us", but that line means different things to different people, especially if they are not aware of the warning signs.

One thing is clear; debt has a price and it will always look for explanation of discrepancies, forgiveness in religious tolerance is a mutating entity admired by many, but practices by the few, and apart from John Wycliffe and William Tyndale trespasses, debt amounts to the same quality of sin.

Bereavement is the human lost of something that has been an integral part of existence, possibly a love one who was all consuming part of life, when they are gone, there is no denying the shock, a person might go for days disorientated and totally incapable of making any sensible decision, reduce to depressive symptoms by the lost of a treasured possession, funeral arrangements are left to those unlikely to show too much emotions, it's time for bankers to feel the acuteness of weeping.

8. **What can governments learn from the subprime credit-crunch banking crisis?**
Government can learn how to come up with simple solutions to stop the decline in housing foreclosure, and provide more liquidity to assist businesses in alleviating the credit crisis. Simultaneously, it can

enforce strict requirements on banks to be more robust in preventing the abuse of gambling away assets. Government can learn above all else, banks cannot be trusted to regulate themselves. With the moral hazard of free market, the government must take the initiative and discourage reckless behavior.
The US economic credit difficulties has triggered immense job cuts and forced millions of people to lose their homes through mortgage payment default, and more people are becoming worried as there appears to be no slowing down of the crisis, the problem has contributed to the breakdown of the family unit in some places, and volatile marriages which were under threat, seemed to be abating with compromises, as many couples come to terms with the lack of money and are divorcing less.
The government is learning from past experience, that through the lack of supervise risk assessment, the credit crunch in banking crisis has severely affected subprime borrowers, and many have lost their treasured homes, along with all their savings, in all honesty, some of the problems that were created in the finance industry, which contributed to the downturn in the property market, was obviously self inflicted, help on by misleading information.
Banks gave people the credit approval to borrow over and above what they could afford to pay back, this was done intentionally, so that loan companies could get a large slice of the commission profit without taking into account the possible dangers; consequently people defaulted on mortgage payments, because they could not afford to make monthly payment.

Life in modern America, and Europe, is not as prosperous as in previous decades, when surplus cash was found in abundant, now people are down on their heel, in collision with earth, executing fewer social events, and been generally careful about what they spent money on, the government is also learning how to take on responsibility of rescuing the banks, knowing that the worst of the financial credit crunch is still to pass the mark of the great depression, so many market analysts believe the consequences could be even more dire.

In sustaining financial stability, FED has cut rates to bolster the finance sector, and safeguard mortgages and other assets, in generating vast amount of liquidity, the stimulus has given the government greater influence in the banking industry, where some banks have been rescued from winding up in administration, and even though the lowering of interest rates is having direct impact on savings account, by reducing the fervency of saving deposits, the government can learn the importance of risk assessment.

The credit crisis has had some strange and unintended consequences on individual's freedom and lifestyle, and the inconsistency of the stock market has continued to give investors the jitters, for example, some business has canceled vast expansion plans, preferring instead to sit and carefully watch the market trend before attempting to reinvest in alternative portfolios. While the government is borrowing their way out of colossal debt, to pave the way for a better global economy, there is a huge price to pay, and repayment will be a difficult subject to tackle.

No one knows when the economy will get stronger, top government politicians are looking at every conceivable way of dissolving the credit problems, the G8 is an economic organization, which meet to discuss the state of the world financial matters. The countries include Canada, France, Germany, Italy, Japan, Russia, the United States, and the United Kingdom.

The responsibility of general hospitality and the settling up of all expenses is placed upon country that holds the presidency, they have the privilege to host the G8 summit, which usually takes place once during the year, and the summit goes on for three days with intense financial matters arising.

Far from the credit crisis abating, in America and Europe, the financial gloom is increasing more with the car industry suffering decline along with the housing property market, so the conclusion that many people have dawn, is becoming painfully embarrassing, on a whole, people believe the government is getting too much of a foot hold in public affairs.

The action of bailing out the culprits does not go down well with the public, and rather than making things better for everyone, they are actually making situation worse, by not severely routing out all the greedy bankers and make them accountable for losses. The only lesson it appears that the government has learn is how to borrow more money to get banks out of the credit crunch.

8. **What can governments learn from the subprime credit-crunch banking crisis?**

Government can learn how to come up with simple solutions to stop the decline in housing foreclosure, and provide more liquidity to assist businesses in alleviating the credit crisis. Simultaneously, it can enforce strict requirements on banks to be more robust in preventing the abuse of gambling away assets. Government can learn above all else, those banks cannot be trusted to regulate themselves. With the moral hazard of free market, the government must take the initiative and discourage reckless behavior.

The US economic credit difficulties has triggered immense job cuts and forced millions of people to lose their homes through mortgage payment default, and more people are becoming worried as there appears to be no slowing down of the crisis, the problem has contributed to the breakdown of the family unit in some places, and volatile marriages which were under threat, seemed to be abating with compromises, as many couples come to terms with the lack of money and are divorcing less.

The government is learning from past experience, that through the lack of supervise risk assessment, the credit crunch in banking crisis has severely affected subprime borrowers, and many have lost their treasured homes, along with all their savings, in all honesty, some of the problems that were created in the finance industry, which contributed to the downturn in the property market, was obviously self inflicted, help on by misleading information.

Banks gave people the credit approval to borrow over and above what they could afford to pay back, this was done intentionally, so that loan companies could get a large slice of the commission profit without taking into account the possible dangers; consequently people defaulted on mortgage payments, because they could not afford to make monthly payment.

Life in modern America, and Europe, is not as prosperous as in previous decades, when surplus cash was found in abundant, now people are down on their heel, in collision with earth, executing fewer social events, and been generally careful about what they spent money on, the government is also learning how to take on responsibility of rescuing the banks, knowing that the worst of the financial credit crunch is still to pass the mark of the great depression, so many market analysts believe the consequences could be even more dire.

In sustaining financial stability, FED has cut rates to bolster the finance sector, and safeguard mortgages and other assets, in generating vast amount of liquidity, the stimulus has given the government greater influence in the banking industry, where some banks have been rescued from winding up in administration, and even though the lowering of interest rates is having direct impact on savings account, by reducing the fervency of saving deposits, the government can learn the importance of risk assessment.

The credit crisis has had some strange and unintended consequences on individual's freedom and lifestyle, and the inconsistency of the stock market has continued to give investors the jitters, for example, some business has canceled vast expansion plans, preferring instead to sit and carefully watch the market trend before attempting to reinvest in alternative portfolios. While the government is borrowing their way out of colossal debt, to pave the way for a better global economy, there is a huge price to pay, and repayment will be a difficult subject to tackle.

No one knows when the economy will get stronger, top government politicians are looking at every conceivable way of dissolving the credit problems, the G8 is an economic organization, which meet to discuss the state of the world financial matters. The countries include Canada, France, Germany, Italy, Japan, Russia, the United States, and the United Kingdom.

The responsibility of general hospitality and the settling up of all expenses is placed upon country that holds the presidency, they have the privilege to host the G8 summit, which usually takes place once during the year, and the summit goes on for three days with intense financial matters arising.

Far from the credit crisis abating, in America and Europe, the financial gloom is increasing more with the car industry suffering decline along with the housing property market, so the conclusion that many people have dawn, is becoming painfully embarrassing, on a whole, people believe the government is getting too much of a foot hold in public affairs.

The action of bailing out the culprits does not go down well with the public, and rather than making things better for everyone, they are actually making situation worse, by not severely routing out all the greedy bankers and make them accountable for losses. The only lesson it appears that the government has learn is how to borrow more money to get banks out of the credit crunch.

9. **Different types of investments to consider in building your financial portfolio**

I want to make it simple for Individuals wishing to invest their savings in selected corporation tailored to meet their requirement, to let you know how to find high quality products, and real source of income streams that can produce fruitful financial revenues. We all agree first of all that everybody wants to make a better standard of living, we do this by the best means possible, scraping and saving up a small part of our disposable income, or we may be fortunate enough to inherit a small legacy, but not everybody is fortunate to find themselves in a position of untold wealth, most people have to work for a living and they are just looking for a way out of the poverty trap, while still others, by deceitful knowledge risk their lives, and the lives of other people to get where they want to be in life, offering large sums of financial rewards for dangerous pursuit, individuals will even borrow with no intention of honoring repayments using delaying tactics with hope of a lucky draw on the lottery or a win on a horse galloping to victory.

Accountability. - Is vital where money is concern; so making an investment for your future requires your full attention because the decisions that you will be making are very important, certain risk will hinge upon those decisions that you will make, so teach yourself simple arithmetic, with plenty of thoughtful consideration for how you spend what you do not earn, living above your means is the easiest way to fall behind in disrepute with your credit card payments, car loan and household repayments, tithing and giving to charitable causes, but by careful budgeting you will see at a glance your income and expenditure, and how to make it even more simpler, your expenditure must not be greater than your income, else you will be negative equity.

Risk.

Investing in common stock is riskier than putting your money in a savings account where you can pay in and withdraw cash on demand, where the befits receive will be poor value, and interest paid yearly is added to your account, ordinary paid up share account is not an applicable way to invest. However, The greater returns investment are related to the stock market's risk, and the stock market is constantly in motion where you expect stock to provide a return on your investment, this includes market timing of buying high and selling low, pushing other potential investors further away from the market. Always keep an eye on the stock market so that you know when to buy a stock that's going up in price, and to sell if stock is going down.

The aim for new buyers is to find the cheapest broker over the life of the transaction, to look after the total transaction cost for buying, holding and selling your shares. And not to lose money foolishly, fortunately there are a couple of steps an investor can take to minimize that risk, by creating Stock Portfolios to

Reduce Risk, and by owning shares of stock in more than one company.

By reducing the risk element to trading retreat, you have a better peace of mind, and minimize the definition of financial risk surrounding the fluctuation of your investment over a long period of time, however, some people are more cautious than others measuring time bases on the amount of cash flow, the higher the duration, or the longer your investment is left to grow the further into the future you will have to look.
Diversification refers to reducing risk by spreading an investment across a number of characteristics. A simple example is "not putting all your eggs into one basket".

Stocks and shares has an element of risk if you don't know what you are doing, The value of investment and the income derived from them may fluctuate and the investor may not receive back the amount originally invested, and the sad thing is that past performance is not an indication that in the future the fund will performed better, so the value of the share prices may go down as well as up.

Managed fund.

May be a safe net for nervous investor where the risk element is low and the fund perform at a stable rate of growth. Pooling
Money from many investors to reinvest in stocks, bond and short term markets. the portfolio manager, will trade the fund's underlying securities, addressing capital gains and losses, then collects the dividends, The investment proceeds are then passed along to all the other individual investors.

Fixed Assets. Are things of value that you own, which could be swap sell or loan out, realistically only tangible assets, are referred to as fixed? Anything that can be uniquely identified can be tracked and accounted for.

Fixed assets normally include items such as property, land and other surplus buildings it can also be motor vehicles furniture, office equipment, lap tops and tower computers, fixtures and fittings, and goes further to owning plant and machinery, These can often receive favorable tax incentives, this too is another source of income investment.

The Types of investment that will offer you real value for your money. Giving benefits and advantages, you will also want your investment to be anchor in a safe harbor in stormy times, not throwing a pardoner, where each person gets a hand each week, and it goes around in a circle until everybody has had a pay out, this can be a quick way of raising money without acquiring any interest, it is rather risky because where there is no legal accountability those collecting the pardoner ship money can become unscrupulous in their behavior, If you are doing this type of savings, you are setting yourself up as a lamb to the slaughter. Sooner or later there is going to be let down and your money will find itself in another person's hand.

My best advice to you would be to get onto the property ladder sooner rather than later, there is no such thing as waiting for the right time in this instance, opportunity is relative to your situation, if you have the knowledge, and there is a proposed acquisition amidst the turmoil of recent days, you can create a passive income stream, outperforming ordinary share account, and will yield higher percentage in the long run, money will always be flowing towards you, by learning the correct way to handle credit uses and its available facilities.

You will be the one standing shortly on top of your, having your finance control of your spending, and not giving dept management the opportunity to charge you so much interest, by you understanding the careful orchestrated purpose of business ethics, your credit cards can be another source of investment solution, not to be use inadvisable for laundry shopping, holidays, and restaurants.

Credit cards, are remarkable simple acquisition of liquid asset readily available when you want, so use them correctly, and your inability to make repayments will be a thing of the past, your credit worthiness is a record of payments made on time, held largely by several companies who will give a report on the strength of your credit worthiness, bad creditors can always repair their file, credit cards is a widespread knowledge of a person's credibility which in modern terms, is just another available income stream. If you are credit worthy then you have the opportunity to make lots more money.

Real estate. Is an increasingly popular way to diversify an investment portfolio? There are typically two ways to invest in the property market. The first is by making a direct investment in a property, such as the home you live in.

That is a positive investment that will yield financial benefits in real terms, and with each successful acquisition you can reinvest back some of the profits that you have gain.

Home ownership is on the increase, and offers a number of potential advantages, the value of house price in many inner cities area have more than trebled in recent years, reflecting the type of financial security that you can gain by owning your own house, it's not throwing away dead money in rent, houses are security for the future, home ownership can give you a higher credit rating, it defines purpose and commitment.

It reinforces caution and lend strength to accountability, its perhaps the largest investment that you will own during your life time, it comes with a degree of problems that will be dissolved over a period of time, including potential tax deductions for a portion of your mortgage payments and a source of equity should you need to borrow money for different financial needs. Second is buying to let, where the property brings in passive income from the rent or lease.

Passive income is an income stream derive from rental property or royalties from selling a book, where money is receive on a regular basis, best example would be network marketing, interest paid from bank, and dividends paid from share holding.

Understanding how money works
Liquid asset may be classified in many ways of accountability, including securities bought and held for sale in the near future to generate more combine income, an asset is a resource controlled by the enterprise as a result of past performance and becomes a reflection from which the future economic benefits are expected to flow to the enterprise account.

Assets have some essential characteristics which in the process of time becomes the embodiment of future benefit that involves a capacity from which financial resources flow into long term investment. Usually Assets characteristics are directly and indirectly referring to cash, which will provide services for essential liabilities.
Cash in turn controls access to other benefits; cash is the most reliable liquid asset, which includes currency, and deposit bank accounts, and negotiable cheques, bank drafts and money order. This converted cash are assets which are continuing turning over in the course of business, multiplying ownership equity.
Assets bring liabilities accounting equation to the economics of the Owners Equity balance sheet, from which we get the sum total of the owner's wealth. But there can be hidden assets which do not appear on the

balance sheet, like in divorce cases where asset are hidden from one spouse to another.

Long-term investments - Investments in securities, such as bonds, and common stock, and takes into account Investments in subsidiaries and spread diversely into affiliated companies. Which may mature into pension funds?

Fixed assets are also called capital assets they are property and buildings held for sale.

The Index. The financial share index is a widely recognized combination of stocks that is representative of a particular market; the index reflects the market that it represents, not the market in general, the number is not important. The most important thing is the percent change over time. This movement up or down gives you an idea of how the index is performing.

When you hear that the market went up or down, you're actually hearing about an index, which is a general indicator of price trends in groups of stocks or bonds. An "index" is a group of stocks or bonds that experts believe collectively represent a larger group of stocks.

The Dow Jones. The Dow tracks the daily gains and losses of stocks from the New York Stock Exchange that the editors consider to be key players in the market and the economy.

Important points to consider

Income streams investment solution.
Purchase a home and add property portfolio
Use credit cards as another stream of income

Diversify business investment into multiple companies
Make good on your credit and mortgage repayments
Fill out your tax returns with a percentage to charity
Budget your income and expenditure
Have an audit trail of all your transaction.

10. **A basic guide to credit**

Adverse credit and default judgments can have severe implications upon your personal enterprises and business application proposals, with disappointing exclusion outcome, obviously most lenders nowadays use a reliable credit checking system to determine your suitability as a borrower. By using this accuracy checking procedure, it clearly eliminates fraud. It does so with an analytical computer generated data base that reviews the matching details of each customer applying for credit. Lenders utilize this method claiming their businesses are dictated by subjected values, and this is how financial institutions carefully work out your risk as a borrower.

Lenders will use various agencies to obtain the information required to process and approve or decline your application for credit. People go into a negative inner denial retreat when they are told that they have failed finance. One of the most striking problems that customer needs to aware of, is that each person is held accountable for updating their credit file. Some will argue that information held against their names are wrongfully imputed giving the overall impression that the person is responsible for the dept. corrective measures are not impossible, but may take some time to amend.

The treatment we receive from financial industry is recognize for what it is, a working agency with different rules and regulations, statistically there is no discrimination if all credit agreements have been honored , but other implications are that most lenders will be reluctant to lend money under normal circumstances to borrowers where the risk are over calculated, however, with the finance market been progressively competitive, there are many other lenders that can be identified with processing successful applications, and they will give loans and even mortgages to customers with adverse credit history. Provided a large enough deposit down payment can be made, the main problem with this solution, is that the rates offered are substantially higher than the usual low risk lender.

However, each lender has a different set of requirements; which in the past regulations have been accused of failing to find the best possible solution for customers and to improve working relationship with the public, welcoming proposals lifted the lid on just specialize treatment, because one lender may overlook some financial credit irregularities, others will focus on two or three payment defaults, the latter, is not by any means damaging if

Surely scrutinize, but will end up been a weak link in the ensuing process, while still another lender ignores court Judgment over a certain age.

The secret really lies in finding the right loan behind the market preconceptions to suit your circumstances, at this stage you may well entertain a broker to come in and help you find what is receptacle, by getting the right broker and you should be able to find a loan to elevate your capital at good interest rates.

However, if you find yourself in the unfortunate position lacking the ability to keep up with payments, something's in this world are almost unforgivable and that goes without saying, if you missed mortgage payments, that delayed abused action alone will incur penalties, that are of a more severe nature. The

implication of that action is regarded by lenders as more critically serious, and interest rates without doubt will come out a lot higher to cover the risk.
Another implication is that most new businesses just starting up will need a bank to transact their affairs from. And of course most banks are happy to offer their services to new customers, however, if any person does not already have an existing account, and they have had credit problems in the past, without making meaningful effort to clear the debt, they will find their application declined, whether the problem is their fault or not, so in all honesty, getting credit could be a difficult challenging job for the first time business person opening an account with sufficient overdraft facilities.
False impression of life does not reflect the challenges poorly handle credit many individual faces, unless they win the lottery, they will never be able to confidently approach lending institutions, Implications with adverse measure will squeezes them out from opening a normal account, especially possessing pending Court Judgments registered against their name, it can be so difficult that banks and building societies will not accept you. Data protection forbids anyone to obtain the information held about another person without first getting the persons permission.

For every individual who uses a credit card or has borrowed money they will have their credit history recorded with the country's leading Credit Reference Agencies; all credit profile details contains the monthly recorded transaction of a person's credit commitments, and their ability make consistent repayment to the assigns agreement, furthermore, each month it is to the borrowers benefit that financial obligations are fulfilled, this information is then is worked out on a monthly score. If a monthly repayment has been met; the score will be zero. If it hasn't; it will be marked one. Failure to make consistent payment will result in further complications and even lessens a person's chance of getting the smallest amount of credit.

If payment isn't met the following month; it's marked two. But it isn't until the third month of non-payment, when it's marked as three, that a default may be recorded. This effectively allows borrowers the occasional financial mishaps before it's entered on their credit history.

With collateral you can still apply for a loan and get it, if you are a house owner, the simple answer is yes. Even if you have a bad credit record lenders are able to offset the risk of a loan against the equity in your property. And while you're unlikely to be offered the most favorable rate, you will still have opportunity to get one foot on the ladder.

11. **Life Insurance: different types**

life insurance provides the kind of financial peace of mind we all need in a world of uncertainty, life insurance addresses the solution of funeral cost and arrangements, reducing the anxiety and stress left to dependents, the situation will inevitable will take place sometime in the future, depending on how much you are insured for, it is recommend that you nudge upwards your indemnity to cover the rising cost of inflation, insurance is a gold mine in catastrophic situations, buyers have the opportunity to go further into the investment sector.

The average person needs enough cover to be sure of security, in the anticipation of unexpected emergency, with joint cover for spouse and your partner available; premium depends entirely on the level of cover you want to suit your personal circumstances. Life insurance falls into different types of category; ultimately they all do the same thing with various degrees of benefits.

Sometimes circumstances will change, and that may require additional premiums, but whatever happens in life, making sure you and your family have adequate life cover and protection you need in the unlikely event of an emergency.

Life insurance is a fixed monthly amount which over the year accumulates to the annual premium, within the contractual term, the policy provides money for your family if you die, and it can also be used to pay off outstanding mortgage, and extend to other debts incurred, usually life insurance is paid out in a lump sum tax free in the event of the death of the policy holder during the term of the specified period of the policy.

Level Life Insurance.

Level life insurance is perhaps the most a simplest form of life insurance. Perfectly designed to pay out a large sum of money should the policyholder die during the term of the policy. Paying the monthly premium remains the policyholder responsibility. Critical illness is another option attached to this policy. With security across the broad a spectrum in mind.

A critical illness.

This option is distinct from private and European medical insurance cover, which pay critical illness plan does not pay for treatment, the sum that you are insured for is payable only on the diagnosis of a critical illness, such as cancer, a heart attack, stroke and kidney failure.

Decreasing Life Insurance.

Decreasing life insurance is a type of life insurance which is designed to cover large capital and interest mortgage in the unlikely event of premature death. Decreasing life insurance will pay out on terminal illness during the term. But the sum will decrease as your mortgage debt reduces. Conditions for paying out would be, Cancer, diagnosis heart attack, stroke and kidney failure.

Everyone need some form of insurance, for travelling abroad on exotic holiday, taking part in jittery love games and career changes, life insurance is perhaps the last thing on a person's mind when they are enjoying themselves, yet when their circumstances have change, tragedy and misfortune will require accountability.

Chapter three

12. **What you need to know about business loans**

Business loans are usually taken out by individuals who plan to own a business, business loans can also be taken out by organizations seeking to the improve their existing business. Business loans are generally used to purchase real estate, refurbishment, machinery and equipment; this will include the office set up, security configuration, and transportation.

Before applying for a business loan, you need to know the wide choice of lenders that are available to fund your capital investment. Get referrals of reputable lenders; take time to do your research.

Financial institution will not grant substantial business loan to any individual or company with bad credit history, however, application for small loans can be a good solution to get people out of poor credit status. Some Unsecured loans obtained, can also be use for business purpose, but higher interest charges will be woven within the contract.

Before applying for a business loan, you need to be absolutely sure you know where you stand with your credit; there are several major credit bureaus that will check every detail on your application. Because of the credit crunch and the state of the economy, by looking at the way the financial market fluctuate, it's a good thing to know what rate of interest you will be making repayments at, for how long, penalties, default and arrangement fee, should all be taken into consideration, if the rate is good, try and get a fixed decision.

Before applying for a business loan you need to know which of the lending institution are more flexibly, shop around to find the most suitable proposition that will be convenient for your business, always make sure that you have proper documentation, business tax returns, along with a recent bank statement showing your income and expenditure consistency. Additional forms of identification will also be required, such as a passport or driving license, and a declaration of other credit cards that you may hold.

The most important piece of information that the financial institution will be looking for, is a business plan, which will illustrate how you will operate the business and make money to pay back the loan. It's essential, that you demonstrate to the lenders define specifics, lenders will grant an individuals and companies business loans, but they first need to ensure how the loan will be repaid. Most banks will take very little risk lending business loans.

A business plan is an informative road map to show how you're going to get to your

Targets. Failure to make a business plan will result in your application being a failure. This applies if you are operating a home business or a corporate industry. Take time to create and maintain a solid business plan. Because you need to know how you are going to run the business before accessing a loan.

In the first two years of operating, it is estimated that 90 percent of small business fail, after risking so much effort and money. This is due largely to many entrepreneurs not having a proper business plan; the result will limit potential earnings.

Incorporated in a business plan, will be the overview which defines the type of business you intend to operate, and the general purpose of the plan, its aims and objectives, along with your product service offering, marketing analysis and management organization, listing the key players and their expertise, if the business plan is primarily to secure a business loan from outside funding, find out in advance what the particular requirements of the financial institution wants to see on the loan application.

Banks will look at certain cash flow revenues and profitability areas, before making any decisions, short term business loans can be repaid over 24 or 36 months, existing business will be required to show current debts and other loan balances, they will also want to see any other investment that is approaching maturity.

Government small business loans are available from the prince's trust, which has an estimated income of over 50 million, with six main type of charitable activity.

I went with my son, to the arranged interview for the prince's trust fund, to obtain the young people’s business programmed loan; the level of expertise was arguably consistent.

mission of the trust is to help young people succeed, by identifying issues and delivering solution which will address the needs, The plan provide money to support young people, it gives community cash award to help set up project that will benefit the community.

You will have to look into obtaining premises and work out a financial budgeting analysis, responsible administration skills will also be taken into account, because the prince's trust takes minimum risk with loans, so in the event of the person not being able to repay the loan, the European investment trust will pay 75% of the outstanding loan.

All business loans have hidden charges with annual fees, closing cost and commission; you need to read the small print before signing the agreement contract. Business loans obtained from other lenders apart from banks, may specialize in diverse solution, financing luxury homes, aircrafts and boats, others may specialize in healthcare property, land and industrial construction.

So my advice to you before applying for a business loan is to get professional advice, before you make the leap, finding out the right information is a simple matter of looking in the right place, even though your mind tells you to surround yourself with a circle of close knit friends and family members. The acquisition of a business loan requires accountability. Lenders have done their home work and they are aware of most eventuality. That's why lenders require a substantial amount of documentation in order to consider a business loan.

13. **Things you need to know before applying for a credit card**

Every day the popular on-line buying with major credit cards at low per cent interest and other new payment methods are becoming a part of the western way of life. At present it is possible to pay almost all your domestic bill on line and even set up direct debits that will automatically make monthly payments where the account holder need not even raise a finger.

While obviously this is not yet fraud proof, the convenience often outweighs any risks that are present. and most people are only too glad to know that the burden of sorting out domestic and other bills are all taken care of, large companies too have made use of this revenue saving convenience.
Looking back on some important things that you need to know about Credit cards before you apply for one, first of all credit cards was first pioneered for the select few who had the means by which to pay back, steadily as the economy picked up, and more money gave customers a greater spending power, the rush for credit took on a new interest.

Now credit cards have become widely accepted in modern society for those even with less than perfect credit rating, The question remains to be answer, and one that many people are asking in the developing world, how can a person with bad credit be a part of these new beneficial systems? What must they do to repair their credit rating? This includes taking their circumstances in consideration, however Today's top credit cards are the envy of most people who are struggling on the ladder to get a good credit rating, and with low APR the prospect is limited, but for the most part this option is unavailable to consumers that have had poor credit history.

But there are new progressive growing markets becoming widely available for those with poor credit rating. Creating an accessible payback solution. And granting bad creditors the opportunity to repair their credit, the schemes are becoming more common and the availability is quickly spreading. The cost of having such a card can work out to be quiet expensive, especially if you go above your spending limit, the penalty charges automatically will be posted onto your account, most credit card companies will charge a handling fee for over stepping the limit.

With all of these new and interesting options open to consumers, there something out there to meet everyone's budget, bad credit cards made widely available will allow just about every individual to take part in our modern economy. With careful budgeting and money management consistent

Repayment effort over a continuous period of time.

Balance Transfers is what credit use to draw customers away to a different company with possible better APR. Companies will offer interest free for a disclosed period of time on your existing debt; they do this in exchange for customers to change their credit card.
There is definitely a minimum amount of payment that you can make each month, and this must be done to avoid charges.
But these only benefits the credit card company, rather than improving your status, because the more debt incurred on credit cards, the less credit worthy you are likely to be. A safe point to consider and put into practice would be how to measure your credit, and stay one step ahead of high charges, the answer is to keep a little less than half of your available credit limit open across all your credit accounts.
Late fees are closely aligned with popular credit cards, this is a deterrent for customers to stay in line and pay their bills on time if they fail to make the minimum payment which is stated on their bill, then the over limit fees will apply if you fail to stay, within your credit limit.
However, by keeping a small balance you will give the credit company the opportunity to increase your balance, many budgeting financial expert will of course tell you the plain advantage, that you should to

pay off your credit card balances as fast as and as quickly as possible.

Credit companies like customers to carry a balance for obvious reasons, and the only real benefit is so they may increase your balance because of this. You'd be amaze how many problems can be solved by having a credit card, so the risk element is, do not carry a balance that will cause you to get behind in payments due to high APR. These are points to watch out for and will save you lots of heartache in the long run.

14. **How to set up a budget**

Budgeting is effective financial management that you put in place, in order to keep track on where money is going, whether you are earning $50,000 a year, or $5,000 a month. It is extremely important that you know how much money you have to spend, and especially where the spending of your money is going.
A budget should have real goals covering long term objectives, with clear and concise understanding of what a person is seeking to achieve, it can be customize to meet current conditions or flexible for maintenance and update, keeping your budget simple to start with then gradually adding categories and outline of income and expenses.
Budget is a purpose plan money spending guide. With this guide, you can organize and control your monthly finances, and be in a better position to set achievable goals, go on vacation or buy a new boat; you can also decide in advance how savings and investment will work for you. A budget can be very simple and flexible to follow, arranged to suit all individual circumstances. It can be done on your computer or manual form.
There are many ideas suggesting how to acquiring more wealth, but spending incorrectly what has been earned, can caused severe financial mismanagement, resulting in the loss of property, leading to more

serious consequences, easy money is getting harder to come by today than it was 10 years ago,

Setting up a budget requires careful planning and preparation, we all have to be extremely careful how we spend our hard earned resource, budgeting is needed to curtail unnecessary spending, along with some smart thinking and juggling of finance to face the future, even in its simplest form, a written budget can break down and divide income into categories of expenditures and savings.

The key to successful budgeting is making your money guide flexible. Certain expenditures are fixed monthly payments that cannot be moved, so payment of those bills should be an inflexible accountability. Which simply means those bills in particular should be paid in full.

By having a budget in place, it allows you to see at a glance, what you have coming in and what you have going out, with this knowledge it gives you power and control over spending, and enables you to plan better for the future. Knowing the exact state of your personal financial affairs, puts you in firm control of them, and allows you to take advantage of shopping bargain opportunities.

In a personal and financial business sense, budgeting can mean flexible estimation of monthly living expenditure based on previous bills and salaries, wages or drawings. If your monthly income is somewhere near $4,000 just for example, you can take away all of your monthly bills from that original figure, the remaining balance after all fixed expenditure has been paid now becomes your household budget.

People care about what they spend their money on, and after a while they will want to know where it all went, fixed bills takes a large chunk, household, family vacation and pleasure also takes up a fair bit,

people who care about their family will always want to put a little aside for savings, this move is important and allows flexibility, because it may not be possible to go on a tropical cruise each year, but the possibility of a two or three weekend breaks in Spain may be affordable.
But the answer is found in something that can make people cope, simple budgeting makes things easier, even when things seemed completely hopeless, and perhaps there will come a time, when the government will run out of good moral thoughts, and resort to fleecing the people for what they can get out of them, it's happening already in many countries.

Be wise, get a budgeting plan in place, and see where all your hard earned cash is going, use what you have got within your power to put a stop to over spending, put all your resources to work, make your assets work for you, use your imagination with energy to focus on the positives, there is plenty of negativity about, without you adding more complex spin to the situation.

Worrying is not going to make things get any better, so make every memory, every impression, a working thought, motivate yourself to higher ambitions, what you are is a great investment to yourself, your family and to the community at large upon earth. However complex the current situation might be the future holds far more intimidating financial worry.
But mankind is a fascinating psychological treasure, and very resourceful with the ability to get out of difficult circumstances, the budget is guide design to produce crucial result, and it allows you to know exactly how much money you have allocated to you, a budget works well for everyone benefit, and having one in place, will almost certainly produce extra money for you and your family to do with as you like.

Chapter four

15. Buying high and selling higher: Momentum investing

The basis for momentum investing is to watch the market stock go up, and speculate that for one reason or another it may come down a little. Momentum investors in general, will quickly recognize this positive trend in the market and capitalize upon it, usually by going after what is rising in value, and selling what is slowly falling.

Momentum investing rejects the notion that they are doing the analysis without some damage caused by their inoperative behavior of rejecting cheaper stock, to pursue the smaller profitable alternative of buying when the market is on the ascent. The tactics used in trading on the stock market are sometimes unfamiliar to the ordinary public, but the strategies are best suited to the investors and the profit margin depends upon a number of leverages, such as the amount of capital that will be required, and the risk assessment that is involved.

Buying higher and selling high seems to make no sense, unless investors have found a way of conquering their betraying habits, by adopting short term strategies to watch the stock market for opportunism, momentum investors has a clinical edge of knowing how to follow market trend, the knowledge is invaluable and guides the investor into the direction where they can trade both ways; short selling the stock when the trend is down is a technical indication of divergence.

Momentum buying when the price is high exhibits the notion of extension analysis, by following the market trend; the strategy is to watch until the effective target has been reached, this momentum strategy is identified as the overall trend of the market increase in rate momentum. This precedence is normally seen in bull market when stock will continue to rise, but investors are cautious to minimize the risk they take.

In the financial trends, movements go up and down, and market prices are sustained over a period of time, the bull market is a term referring to the optimism of investors interest, in the movements of the market anticipating substantial capital gain, a bull run is like the bullying behavior of a herd of bulls, gorging upwards with their horns with respect to the market or particular commodities.

The bear market presents no surprises here, to avoid further loses investors are motivated to sell, on the way down, because of increasing pessimism, bear market is a substantial decline in prices with negative feelings feeding on itself, the market movements are caused by speculation, and expectation changes the environment, the momentum investing operates both ways with a segment of investors trying to outsmart the market.

Some people will take the view that momentum investing is just pure luck, while others place it in the category of more losses, especially if as we have seen, investors buy high and sell even higher they are investing with psychological and emotional feelings;

the law of probability is possible, but the law of average estimate a greater loss.
This can be measure when share prices decline over a period of two monthly terms, bear market is heading towards a state of stagnation with recession inevitably following, the great recession in 1929 stock market crash, spelled the end of the bull market, and in addition to all other plausible trends, the losses continues to be the bench mark the market used to gage all recession trends, today's recession is expected to bottom out, when the bear market rallies in the Dow Jones share index.
In China, Soaring interest have risen again in production output, because since the beginning of last July, production in raw materials slowed down drastically, falling back almost 20% on previously held figures, pushing companies into the bear market, however, recently there is a new appetite in production, and commodity bulls is soaring with high expectation even with inflationary pressure, the demand for products is far outstripping the present supply. Momentum may not be a wisest choice of investment at this present juncture of timing.
The reason of course is that the Chinese have a very strong and determine mind, set upon toppling inflation, even though it is at the risk of the economy not picking up as quickly as they would have liked, due largely to the cost of modernization which is still an outstanding national debt, demands are high for China, to maintain their success story following on from the Olympic games.

But whenever the market is in decline, the demand falls short and more caution is exercised, in a bull market, prices go up and bubbles are burst, the search for momentum strategies requires the use of careful judgment, lest we forget that the market trend has a changing sequence, venture at your peril.

Buyer's incentives

Selling a house in a an increasingly depressing market requires more than cosmetic decoration if the property is to appeal to interested parties, buyers will make conscious effort to look at all available houses that are within their budget, it helps if certain incentives were already in place when viewing has a been made possible.

Due to the share prices of house builders plummeting, as a result of the industry underperforming, we see the widening slump of the economy throwing up diverse ways for companies to create additional revenues, developers are trying to lure new buyers into the market by offering what appear to be lucrative incentives, and I suppose the idea sounds really fantastic.

Tempting offers of exotic holidays and mortgage subsidy, on face value appears to be clever thinking, but it pays to do your mathematics, if what they are offering really amounts to something that is beneficial to the buyers, and not just a condition for developers to make extra profit, right across the country, we seeing more frequent glossy averts with juicy temptation for buyers to consider.

The free giveaway of new fully fitted kitchen and customize extras, such as plasma television, and music surround sound system, furnishing and legal fees, the inside sale information is nothing more than a trick by developers to inflate the selling price, at first, it all sounds like buyers are getting something good, just for their signature on the contract, however, on closer inspection., these artificial giveaways seek only to lure first time buyers into thinking they are being well looked after.

Before signing any contract on house purchase, it is advisable to check that these tempting offers are legit, showing transparency over what you are getting as opposed to the original sale price of the house, if the juicy giveaway is expected to be $15,000. And the recorded sale of the house is $240,000 the true value of the property is only $225,000. If the juicy giveaway total is not deducted the price of the property has been inflated.

Banks and lenders are becoming more cautious by exercising greater restriction on the amount they will lend on a property, after carefully examining the surveyors report on the property, lenders will come to a decision about the amount they will lend potential borrowers, of course this position makes it a little bit more difficult for first time buyers, to get on the lucrative homeowners ladder, so while the market is tight, incentives needs to be more than juicy tempting offers, they need to be relevant.

The tough economic conditions has made the acquiring a mortgage very difficult, and even harder for first time buyers to bridge the gap, unless better guidelines are given, pointing out the pitfalls, and the opportunities, greed will still continue to increase, and make fools out of the unsuspecting buyers, some form of structure needs to be in place to limit these kinds of negotiation with tricky fire crackers envelope within the deal.

Residential purchases has always been an area of ethical dealings, with customers looking forward to getting lasting value for their money, now developers have turned a new chapter in pilfering, and are been force to off load juicy incentives, that are really only a smoke screened, price reduction and incentives should go hand in hand, and not bogus deals, shading the truth with bright ideas of exuberant artistry.

Meet the bedrock of housing stability

The value of house prices has fallen from what they were originally valued at, leaving loan payers with very large sums of money lost.

Economics and the neutrals watched and waited to hear the announcement, of the greatest financial bailed out offered by the US treasury, in taking over the crippling debts of Fannie Mae and Freddie Mac, two of the biggest names in the mortgage housing sector, but the dilemma for one corporate business association, presents another opportunity for government seizure.

Spare a thought, for the way the housing market is going, conditions are favorably to savers rather than for home buyers, making the prospect not particular good for those facing a bleak winter of financial uncertainties, to buy a house now requires a large deposit to sure up the loan application, but if after purchase completion, but years gone by, Fannie Mae and Freddie Mac, the bedrock of housing stability, would have made the acquisition possible.

However, if buyers are unable to make regular loan repayment, it won't be long when the doors are closed in foreclosure for those unable to meet their mortgage obligation, and the keys of the vacant kingdom are handed to another occupier at reduce rates.

Hence, the government is the new occupier, becoming the financial underwriters of the mighty fallen housing entrepreneurs, Fannie Mae and Freddie Mac, the surprising of course, was unprecedented, never in history was a company bailed out of the darkest hole, it was a move that characterize the importance of the housing market.

This was no ordinary speculative bombshell, hearing about the dismal news about the mortgage pioneers that are known worldwide, Fannie Mae and Freddie Mac, is the twin engine of mortgages, consortium giants woven into the fabric of American society.

For years they have been the bed rock of stability, and it is great news to hear that the treasury has intervene to rescue the giants that were in financial disarray, home owners have stroke the pains of displeasure over the past ten years paying for houses that are well over valued, some people have not yet reap the fruits of their reward, while others perched nervously on the pinnacle of trade winds.

Having mortgaged themselves to the hilt, and as a result, home owners are having negative equity, which simply means, the value of the house price has fallen from what it was originally valued at, leaving loan payers with very large sums of money to fork out each month on properties that are now well under what they initially were.

With the housing slump continuing, mortgages are not worth a great deal today as they were back in 2006, when the slump started to take affect the economy, trade deficit came into play, and speculation of a steady stream of income was encouraging, but as the oil prices increased, the value of houses began to drop 5% at first, by 2007 another 15% of the value of houses fell sharply, and the knock on effects took place with further increase in food and energy prices.

However, Fannie Mae and Freddie Mac remained optimistic that they were able to weather the storm, with history on their side, it was hard to see them not pulling through, and plug the gaps with holes to stop the leakages, it goes to show that we cannot take any financial matter for granted, it may have happen prematurely, but their inept action proved there undoing, and consequently they lost more than a truck loan of cash.

Along with their previous consistency in providing more than half the mortgages in the US, their reliable reputation has been ripped to threads, the company share prices took a massive tumbling for the worse, unlike any other mortgage companies, who may have had other investment to sure up their securities, Fannie Mae and Freddie Mac had lost so much equity, their balance books was in a total mess, eventually under the unbearable weight of lost revenue, the twin engines stalled, and a rescued mission from the treasury had to be quickly enforced to prevent complete disaster.

The world at large was aware of the reputation that Fannie Mae and Freddie Mac had develop over the years, but not as closely align to their situation, as those home owners who are paying back over the top higher rates on loans, and seeing the possibility of foreclosure starring them smack bang in the face, defeat is not an easy thing to accept, but if they can walk away from near disaster with half their integrity and dignity intact there may be hope of a great revival, but it's doubtful the way the market is at the moment, there is a sense of uneasiness in the atmosphere.

Cutting interest rates has stimulated the market a little, and banking opportunities are holding steady, it appears that we will always be going back to the economy to examine pressing mortgage issues, $350,000 houses have plummeted in value, to around 25% off, in some states the drop is worrying, working home owners need more of a stimulus package to see a rejuvenated surge in house value, the deficit that they are facing with their mortgage payments can so easily be blamed on Fannie Mae and Freddie Mac, who sold most of these mortgages in the first place.

There is no doubt, that the lenders guidelines used to assist in applying for mortgage loans has worked successfully over the years, but since 2006, working family income has dropped by inflation adjustment, with even worse fears to come, in the way of job losses, and the disadvantage unfairness dished out to first time buyers who are trying desperately to get on the housing ladder.

Economists, fearing an economic slide may wipe out more stock prices, are looking at ways to assist loans payers especially those obligated to Fannie Mae and Freddie Mac, but it is coming up to decision time, when they may have to decide whether it is worth selling up and cutting their losses, or press on through the stagflation hoping for the best. The current problems encountered by those bearing up to negative equity, may be an uncompromising dilemma for some, but for others, it may be a passport investment opportunity

Foreclosure and repossessions

Foreclosure will happen to more people this year than last year, many more families, businesses and entrepreneurs will lose their homes, this will be largely due to late payment, when homeowners cannot make payments on time for their mortgage, and fall behind with payments over six to nine months, under the contract of financial obligation, the lending institution has the rights to repossess the property, some banks are a little more flexible than others, depending on the relationship the borrower has with the bank, they will try to give you time to make good on your promise, but the paper work usually will have started.

As a result of inability to make payments on time, borrowers have defaulted on their agreement with the lending institution, it leaves no other alternative but to shut out the borrower, foreclosure is to terminate all existing rights of the homeowner covered by a mortgage contractual agreement, and reposes the property, in the ensuing process, the estate becomes the absolute property of the lending institution.

The rise in unemployment and soaring inflation points to a downward beat, wobbly assessment that the financial sector is experiencing is showing how unstable the economy is, with news of the cost of living getting from bad to worse, many individuals today are expressing their concern leading to the entrance of recession.

The longer this trend goes on, the more worried householders become, many are afraid of losing their homes, but some homeowners have put in an emergency plan to avoid lost, seeing the value in property decline, the painful and adjustment that the economy is going through, this reality is causing people to rent out their homes rather than sell at drastically reduce prices.

The higher the prices are in the shop, the more the gloom deepens, fuel products are far more expensive than a year ago, the economic climate is worrying with rising unemployment and spiraling personal debt, people are finding it hard to pay their credit cards, make full payments on their mortgages, and keep up with car loans payments.

Mortgage payments are the biggest concerns, followed by rent, domestic bills and taking vacations, rising inflation has put paid to all the good times, it's now a time to save with pennies from heaven, and say a little prayer at the same time, what we had taken for granted a few years ago, we are now paying back for it, with the add on aggressive increase in price of household gas and electricity, foreclosure and repossessions are imminent.

With all the jittery nerves hanging, someone has to tie up the loose ends, especially when billions will be wiped of the stock market, this will plunge long standing companies into severe danger, survival will depend largely upon many gearing factors, nerves of steel, consistency, flexibility, new market, investment, sophistication, commitment, quality, we give the expression that we are concern, but our determination tells another story.

but while the job market is weak, and warning of grimmer times ahead, than just a flat economy, there is a glimpse of satisfaction for existing property owners who can find the guts to struggle on, as long as firms don't try to force through price increases, in constructing new homes, wages will remain steady, giving a flat economy, and declining domestic demands will keep inflation low.

But when mortgages and housing cost collapse, we crumble like a pile of bricks embracing the pains of the economy, our thinking even becomes negative like the financial institutions, showing unpleasant instability, rather than engage and reaffirming our stance, widening our grip to developing new ideas for survival, notice how the eastern states are prospering, they are obviously doing something well, or putting up with a little inconvenience, that we in the west find hard to accept.

However, over the next 12 months we will all be facing some enormous challenges, foreclosures and repossession is set to double from the present figure, with many people walking away from their homes, unable to pay the high mortgages, in the UK alone, it is estimated that over 40,000 homes repossession will take place this coming year.

But you get a feeling that the American economy will stay flat ahead of the game, the US is showing signs of a less false economic gloom than in Europe, and while the country is going through this adjustment, it's looking very much that they can cope better with the strain.

Repossession also opens the door of opportunity for others to purchase at a reduce price, so when one door closes another opens with booming interest, one persons misfortune is another person's opportunity, some people have refuse to say there was even a crisis, were they blind or just oblivious? Some have plainly said they budgeted better and put up strong resistance.

So while the credit crunch is taking such a bruising effect upon others, not all of us are affected, we can diversify, and uphold some of the severe measures, with a stiff code of ethics, and still have serious concerns for the economy. This reality is self regulation, reaffirming our status, supervising our assets, and taking control of our own destiny rather than leaving things to a monopolizing chance.

16. **Surviving the economic crunch**

Radical measures are needed to survive the credit crunch and to get us out of this terrifying financial dilemma, where the equity market just keeps on free falling, and the economy is surrendering to recession, the almighty dollar will rally a little help on by sheer aggression of the fed's monetary respite, but this powerful and worrying situation will continue well on into the future.

Only a few years ago investors thought interest rate cuts was the answer to our problems and guaranteed financial stability, it may have worked back then, however, today we are dealing with a new concept of credit. And it's called credit crunch, the economic prospect ahead is terrifying, unconsciously powerfully worrying. With the coming recession making the future looking rather gloomy our best effort seemed to be bringing negative response, reducing our disposable income to a minimum. The harsh reality is that things will get much worse before they get better, best way out at the moment, is for everyone to tighten their belt and prepare a for a rough ride to safety.

Countries never wanted to play rough, nor did they ever thought they had to against their will, but today's economic aggressive market requires no holds barred, and policy holders have become engaged in a far from elegance pace setting game, everyone across Europe knows that the US financial system which for many years was reliable is now facing a crucial meltdown, this may not be for the most the worst scenario nor do we hope it will be the ultimate outcome, but there are fears and edgy nerves coming apart at the seams.

The likely ending is that the US investment bank will be bailed out giving a strong recovery to the weaken balance sheet, so investors will not see the pressure on liquidity, a day is a long time in the finance world, think what damage a bad week could do towards the dollar, rescue packages will raise some very big questions, until now the answers are limited, but it’s possible to argue the point about where authorities have got things wrong.

How could Northern Rock collapse so dramatically stemming from the bank of England s failures to inject vital liquidity?

And it’s strange behavior, along with the ignorant unwilling decision not to cut interest rates? Also we need to take into account that the authorities seemed unwilling to some degree to find a resourceful buyer, and of course the government also had a big part to play, because they showed immaturity in their lack of insight to bail out Northern Rock from the their distress. Injecting reserve liquidity sooner would have stopped the jitters and guaranteed investors their deposits were safe.

Taking decisive decisions during dark financial days is typically what we pay our fund managers to do, they are in the perfect position to look out for the best possible returns on investors' money help along by the normally reliable system, when these avenues fails then optimism goes a drift, replace by growing skepticism, although interest rates have fallen along way and people seemed to have more spending power, there is absolutely every reason to be cautious, because of the ever growing nervous effect, which can so easily trigger off financial stability.

Loans will become harder to come by, and potential home buyers have to think twice about their repayment. Because value for money is what everyone is looking for, but the financial institutions are looking to make a little extra. So caution is the answer to all investment plans. Payments will always go up because interest rates are not stable, everyone who has a mortgage will feel the squeeze, and many people will lose their best assets that they have worked for over many years, try as they may, people are going to lose their jobs, homes and business, so it's important to learn how to manage debt. When rates payment goes up good budget control must be introduce into family financial plan.

The time for stupid mistakes are over, because as we have all been witnessing how the us dollar has virtually plunge to a new low, this is a worrying situation, to see the doomsday of our economy unable to strengthen itself against previously weaker economy.

The Yen's strength is particular applauded, the Japanese astonishing currency is control by the central bank and they have the market on their side, much preferring the Yen to the ever shrinking dollar

which is quickly heading down the creek without a paddle.
We are witnessing a breakdown in the financial institution on a mass scale that does not give any simple answers, rate cuts are not helping the US dollar, this is a credit crunch, the best that we can hope for, is a massive injection of foreign investment and I am presuming that we will take the safe route perhaps to offset against rocky times ahead, the world is a more intelligent place now and people are not easily fooled, they are quickly wising up to comparable decisions and need answers to the wealth of funds which has distort reality.

And if the e markets continue to nose dive it will lead to huger loses and in turn contribute to long term instability, leaving no alternative but for tax payers to reluctantly foot the damages and clean up the mess. It is coming a crunch when all overall financial review is drastically needed; there is no quick fixed solution as we witness the breakdown within the financial institutional system.

Banks have been increasingly forced to cut back on lending, overdrafts and credit limit have been slash to the minimum and the power that central bank possess has become steadily ineffective, even though the markets has created cash in the pockets of many householders, the turn up is without much impact, the projection for the future, is that The economic strain will continue to sit down harder upon all of us.

Risk assessment

Risk assessment is a careful examination of supervision to protect the security of investment, by looking at ways to reduce the possibility of harm to people, it is the practical assessment of identifying where hazards could significantly be reduce, the aim is to make sure that individuals are not at risk from the lack of supervision, by taking all the necessary precautions to cover damage limitations, in decision making and evaluation of the work force, leading to all areas which requires accountability.

Just about everything that we do requires a certain amount of risk assessment, whether we be at home, or the work environment, the heart of the matter is the workforce, industries, individuals, savings , investment, performance task, institutions, avoiding catastrophes, management regulators, some of these areas capture the programming of transitional possibilities, in the banking industry the review of assets would be high on the list, evaluating record finding and lost revenues, the risk assessment would decide what measure would be needed to cover adequately any possible violation.

Many banking institutions in the past, have failed to manage their risk assessment program properly, consequently the result of their errors has made them look shambolic, and this failure has resulted in the public losing confidence in the banking sector, for creating the economic crisis that the world at lager is in, we must now repair the damage that has been maliciously done, and create awareness of the need for better risk assessment approach, by taking into account the type of business we want to see improving, when there is better understanding of risk assessment, the chances of avoiding financial catastrophe will be limited.

This may become the new path of financial economics essential for growth, in developing more sensible approach to tackle the subject, and apply accountability to oversight and see that improvements are working measurable, the new method for risk elimination will safeguard jobs and underpin the viability of the business.

In management consultation, elements of the present inept banking system will need to be replaced, or all the financial institution will continued to be discredited, decisive decision is now radically needed to sort out the mess, even though there are some validity in the basic areas of risk assessment, which is still working quiet well, previous inadequate supervision only have a limited time before been exposed for insufficiently lacking protection, but fresh investment in overhauling old techniques will give the financial sector more innovations.

We all know that financial products, such as long term investment, ordinary savings account, fixed assets, pensions, share values, new home purchasing, property ownership, plays a major part of our lives, so let's face it, these are the prime areas that can contribute to the creation of wealth, which is then used in several ways to defray expenditures and acquire the basic necessities for survival.

If the possibility of hazards is definitely high, the need for control measure must also be in place, even after taking all precautions, the likely elements of risk may still remain, the hard part comes in deciding whether it is medium high or low.

The new approach to risk assessment, is by first trying to identify where the fault was? What supervision was in place if any? what level of accountability was permitted for decision making?, if having identify where the problem lies, we must then come to the judicious understanding of reasons for such management failures, embarrassment must be taken out of the equation, and ignorance be replaced with workable models , that provides effective checks and balances against banks making the same mistakes.

The financial risk cannot be understated, because the world economy is at risk, and failure to find the solution and implement them now, will caused greater difficulties in the future, and be more painful as well as damaging to the fabric of society, the world needs to enjoy long periods of growth and low financial incumbencies, volatility is wrong assumption of permanent, and miscalculated errors benefits no one, lease of all the banks.

When fundamental errors occurs in financial industry, it gives cause for concern, in how to avoid another failure of risk management, the risk management models used in banks were generally based on simplified assumption, that the market would somehow correct itself over a period of time, following normal statistical approach, which implied the probability of losses would be extremely low, however, they were ignoring the aspect of financial history repeating itself.

There were not enough security to bolster complex pricing of the housing market, which crashed horribly; such products sold to sub-prime customers warranted a better overall guarantee. If the banks had considered that the risks for taking on projects with limited equity, they should have had other diverse portfolio to sure up the short fall, for which the existing control measures were inadequate.

Risk management has to prove adequate for reasons familiar with hazard behavior and economic emphasis on quantitative models, ignoring experience was a major risk in the banking sector, management failed to interpret the dangers objectively, when they were overlooked potential hazards, instead of applying a better control over monitoring toxic debt to avert the undervalue risk, they failed to apply independent checks and balances, that were needed to cover the capital balances.

And as profits quickly started to dwindle, time was not on their side for making smart recover, although some bank managers had made their escape through the back doors with heavy pots of gold, those left to carry the can were doubtless very ashamed of new developments, and the stock market made sure the world knew what was going on, pessimism contributed largely to the stock market crash, money dried up with credit frozen on all fronts, business found difficult to survive the crunch.

When assessing the risk of new products, the driving force behind the business is to root out possible errors, between undervalued products and deficiencies in negative equity, regulators must be aware of the risk banks are taking when qualifying loans, positively looking at the risk management boundaries, although the idea appears to be irritating, it is important to safe guard investment, and subjective elements in market behavior, soft qualitative approach should run harmoniously alongside hard and fastened statistical rules equally as accountable.

The financial world must embrace new strategy in combating nervousness, with powerful mathematical techniques, by introducing new complex initiatives which will readily capture the market in bear season, attracting more business and give more confidence to investors; the key is to combine weakness with strength, practical solution with responsible behavior.

Each section of banking must be accountable, risk management was develop long ago by investment bankers that knew the value of control in the gradual rise to greatness, this modern breed of bankers wants to be millionaires within one week of taking office, there are no surprises here, the only problem remained unanswered, was why were they allow to get away so freely?

17. **Types of investment you can buy**

Life insurance is a fixed monthly amount which over the year accumulates to the annual premium, the contractual terms provides money for your family if you die. It can also be used to pay off outstanding mortgage, and extend to other debts incurred; usually life insurance is paid out in a lump sum tax free in the event of death taking place during the specified period of the policy.

Life Insurance is not a betting group showing revenues falling and performance lodged in poker division, if gambling is a mugs game then having life insurance is a cert. looking at recession trudging along with its bumpy ride, showing a downside to the economy, many people are presently struggling to meet most of their obligations, but insurance should be one of the first things paid on the monthly budget check list.

So why do we need insurance? The simple answer is, relative safe haven, you as an individual, cannot underestimate the value of having life insurance, because it will give you security and peace of mind should the worst happen. Life insurance does several things but mainly it protects your loved ones against future financial hardship, it is also invaluable advice that you can either choose wisely to accept or foolishly ignore, the cost, the length, and the benefits, are the basic points you should consider, when taking out a policy, the folio group description then breaks down into different types of insurance.

Sometimes our circumstances will change and that may require additional premiums, but whatever happens in life, making sure you and your family have adequate life cover and the protection you need in the unlikely event of an emergency. If you have as I suspected, some kind of life insurance, it will be a fair amount of value to you, and there are advantages to be gain when you analyzes the underline benefits and put your life into real context.

Partly because life insurance provides the kind of financial peace we all need in an uncertain world, and it addresses the solution of funeral arrangements for our dependents which inevitable will take place in the future, depending on how much you are insured for, it is recommend that you nudge upwards your indemnity to cover the rising cost of inflation, insurance is a gold mine in catastrophic situations, and buyers can get themselves further into the investment sector. And find companies with upbeat records trading with impressive growth.

Professional people are prone to relocation, living the dream and taking exotic

vacations, traveling abroad, taking part in jittery games and career changes, life insurance is perhaps the last thing on a person's mind when they are enjoying themselves, yet when their circumstances have change, tragedy and misfortune can also come knocking in the most unusual circumstances, in bed, on a aircraft, shopping, walking home, danger in huge numbers without etiquette is always just lurking around the next corner ready to squeeze the life blood out of our strutting existence.

Likewise, moving houses involves hard work, starting a family too is even harder, and there is little to suggest that everything will go right, changing your job is vital for independence and financial reasons, so it's a really good idea to review your life insurance and protection needs, financial consultants are always available to advise you on exactly how much cover you should have and the type of insurance you would need for income protection or even critical illness, policies should be arrange accordingly to suit your budget.
There are many types of insurance that you can buy, they are widely available take on your descriptive personal choice, starting with cautious defensive decision to take control of your destiny, if you can control your own importance, you can then prepare for a better future.

Level Term Assurance, are the fixed premiums paid for a number of years, normally between ten and forty years, then if any fatalities should happen, a full payout is guaranteed at any point during the term, provided full payments have been made to the company on time.
Then we have Increasing Term Assurance, which is not as popular as level Term, but does almost the same work and just as affective, the security comes with additional cover providing substantial peace of mind to combat inflation rises.

Increasing Term Assurance is also quiet good, in that it gives adequate peace of mind by providing cover which as the term suggested, increases every year, this policy is offered without the need for any medical, but it should not be something that is forced upon a person, but it is needed only as individuals may require for extra cover in line with increases in their income.

Decreasing term assurance, at first sounds crafty, because the payout reduces over the cover period at a flat fixed rate each year. The aim of this plan is to provide cover for the period you have chosen, and for the company to pay the lump sum if you die during the period of cover, but the amount of cover

Will decrease over the chosen period. And importantly, the risk factor suggest that if you fail to keep up with payments, after thirty days your plan will lapse and no benefits will be payable, that clause more or less applies to all the groups. This plan has no cash in value; you should ensure that the term of the plan is long enough to cover the term of your mortgage.

Mortgage Protection Assurance, this type of insurance is realistic and puts a delicate value on your life, it works for you in line with what you owe, because what you owe to the building society decreases with the passing of time as you are paying off your mortgage, well so does the amount of cover and the premium, so this is where the lump sum reduces in line with the outstanding mortgage balance over time.

In every 24 hours there are thousands of claims processed; most of these claims have resulted from traffic accidents. A solicitor representing you will bring a claim for compensation to an insurance company following the event of a serious injury to either yourself or a family member. Claims are processed from the result of fatal traffic collision, fatal road accidents, drivers involved in hit and run. So do yourself a big favor, shop around, and take out some life insurance, it will be worth the risk in the long run.

What is the price of urgency?

In a sense that I am going to get something g out of every day, when the fire alarm goes off people think urgency is as the result of a false alarm, so they remained in their hotel room, until an everlasting bang comes knocking at the door, and it's not always for rescuing, but in an emergency situation, there are all kinds of survival possibilities.

from climbing out the window to taking the emergency exits, as the economic tension builds up, and the housing market takes another turn we hope for the better, investors have breathe a reflected sigh of relief, although it may only be short live.

Fannie Mae and Freddie Mac have succeeded in delaying the inevitable, having been bailed out of their drowning financial worries, by the US treasury, because the twin engines had stalled, however, the downturn is still active and the difficulties will not go away over night, but the move will delay stay of execution, and housing prices will continue to fall back on last year's figures, to at least another 10% down, sympathy must be for those mortgage payers currently languishing with negative equity, paying back more than what the house is worth.

It is always a wise move to buy as cheap as possible in the eventuality of things not going to plan, your investment will remain safe, management is about taking control of money matters, hence the urgency to make good on your field of expertise, know your strength and invest in other emerging markets, because if you leave your eggs in one basket, you may ended up with little or having nothing, the possibility may even arrived where you will just have to walk away from the home that you have build up.

The Federal Reserve made cash available quick in rescuing the perishing, taking the opportunity to snatch the twin mortgage giants from pity, duty demanded it, what an incredible stark contrast to the bungling efforts of the British treasury, who had ditheringly made plans to bail out Northern Rock only after the horse had bolted through the gates.

When our economy started to slow, Fed cut interest rates, despite the concerns for inflation, banks held steady, so what is the price of urgency? It is the result of very smart thinking, to rescue the perishing, and care for the dying, which does not take five months to revise, not when the apparent disaster is starring economy right in the face. Washington steps in to take control of Fannie Mae and Freddie Mac, throwing out life line for mouth savoring effect.

European funds have had a hard time this year, speculation for next year are already in place, with so many big names been affected, now is not the time for complacency, but for urgency to increase tactics, and observed where the cheapest market is breaking ground at the moment, the financial revenue, possibly lies within the borders of enemy territory , Russian stock is cheap at the moment, with 20% speculative growth expected in 2009, hedge funds are looking to set up investment in Russia , commodities stock make up more than half stock market, and the government tax taken from oil companies, will depend on the price of oil.

Seeing the opportunities and taking them is a greater vision than grieving over the hazards that are out there, sometimes a person just has to go with gut emotional determination in order to succeed, the risk are there for losses and gain, and very often people do not see them, because they are more concern about the dander, success is driven by determination in the face of danger, and time is running out for the us economy to make good.

Other countries have not fully caught up, but just look in the rear mirror and you will be shock to see close encounters of a different kind, they are almost upon our heels, it's a rude awakening not to panic or do anything frenetic, but doing something useful is better than doing nothing, make a move to invest wisely in other markets, because soon many more houses will shut their doors and go into foreclosure.

The government was slow in seeing the crippling financial effect of mortgages spiraling out of control, with no back up plans were hardly in place, so they now quickly follow the path of Northern Rock, but how long for? Banks are in danger of getting sucked into funding inability, so who will justify the need to protect investors and depositors , will banks be rescued by their share holders, as the world moves faster, so does the economic stronghold with no holds barred, organization have to equip themselves better to deal with the severity of the crash that is coming.

Seven years of famine, Pharaoh had his Joseph to plan, prepare and present a working a agreement, Fannie Mae and Freddie Mac were bailed out this time by an executive hand out, rescuing them from slaughter, the margin for risk puts assets and premium still at a greater risk, the hour of dilemma is upon us, urgency in real financial activity must increase with our sense of timing.

In some peoples mind, Northern rock is still a ship with holes taking in water, and there is a strange sense that something more firm is needed, to keep investors and creditors not trembling with nightmares, so they are looking with wide range powers to disenfranchise stakeholders in the failing bank, by overriding contractual rights and nullifying various terms of securities.

The US and UK markets are very different, the policy options available to London differs to that of Washington, the us has responded to the housing crisis by rescuing Fannie Mae and Freddie Mac, twin engines that consistently fund most American mortgage they are the bedrock of housing system, guaranteeing $12 trillion in outstanding mortgage debt. But since housing prices have been falling back during the past two years, the giant undercapitalized has exposed themselves to huge losses, leaving the twin engines grinding to halt, until Hank Paulson the treasury secretary made his proclamation.

His swift action over the weekend may have stop the cruelty that was awaiting around the corner, well done to the us treasury , they were quick to spot an opportunity, and complete the rescue mission, it is the largest state financial intervention known on record, but it took guts and urgency to respond to the market turmoil.

19. **Planning for your financial future**

We are acutely aware that investment and savings are critically important to help shape our financial future, a task which should not be taken lightly or ill advisably, because in later years may prove to have serious consequences maintaining lifestyle standards, however, if we approach the subject objectively with honest appraisal and sensible review of personal assets leading cautiously to some degree of exposure into the financial sector, where individuals should look with interest for advise to assist their retirement agenda and prepare some financial enumeration plan. It's only human nature to want to participate in something that may be profitable, and no one wants to feel like they're missing out on profitability.

Financial Planning should encompass long term savings for the future, the most secure option is investment in a house, but if this solution is not possible, then other investment and regular savings is your next best bet, which could be taken as a simple accumulating method that can be achieve with

regularity, base upon consistency and of course taking some consideration for individuals who are on low income, finding a plan to suit their needs will in the long term be worthwhile, so one sure way out from the retirement disaster is to bypass the suppressing anxiety of current despondency and find the avenue that will cautiously engineer a path to debt free realization, by been consciously driven to resolve financial indifference's and meticulously organize personal finances to enhance the later years.
it's hardly surprising to hear friends declared how bad a grip they have upon their finances, many people have just barely made it thorough into their thirties and forties without starting a pension or even putting aside some form of managed fund savings for future emergency, in our society, there are individuals that have no inheritance upon which to build, and they live on the fearful demising edge of reality, lacking resourceful measure in which to obtain a decent standard of living, and having no adequate skills to fall back upon, the possibility of retraining has become such a daunting phenomenon, a venture hardly worth entertaining.

In a world plague by get rich quick schemes, lottery enchantments, casino poker games, quizzes masters, bingo nights, the list goes on, drinking away hard earned funds, playfully on the crest waves of building your hopes up with false illusions, there are without doubt some exception, each week a few hundred lucky

winners are apportioned the luxuries of winning a minor fortune, but the majority of ordinary people live without any long term investment, and to an even greater degree, most people live from day to day without any forms of savings to call on, they are still struggling to make ends meet each month, without help from their credit cards and large bank overdrafts. this practice may even go on to fulfillment in later years, Maybe you have found yourself in that category and are wondering what you can do to improve situation.

Living on the edge may be exciting but thoughts of the future can also be petrifying, because most people are not putting nearly enough into their pension in order to finance long term retirement, meaning the future holds scary long hours of unnecessary work in the weary toil of financial pressure cocker, where in some countries under discipline sanctions, food embargo is going to create havoc in what is already a hostile environment, millions of people are going to need to work much longer and live more humble existence in their old age.

So depending upon your sex and age, if a person has been working since the age of 21years old and contributing to company pension scheme, by the time they have reached 65 years of age they are still expected to live another 20 years and possible longer, therefore I believe we need sound financial advice on how to prepare ourselves for the twilight years with an education in money management.

The long term solution clearly lies in educating our children and grandchildren with the basic understanding of budgeting, and learning the importance of consistent regular saving to alleviate the consequences of being overly indebted, if individuals start early their savings and investment are unlikely to descend back into the desperate level to which we have plunge today, but what about the millions who have gone already through the school gates, is there any hope?

The governments answer to this mismanaging is woefully inadequate, they are not that interested in personal matters, unless it has direct relevance to paying some kind of taxes, but examining the possibility for those on lower income, if government were interested in setting up financial advise line, they could create generic financial service without risky instability, but link up with the network of banks and other financial services where private investors could be invited to promote a rescue package.

What are the implications? Well for a start, financial

Advisers would be paid by commission or bonus fees, and they would be helping people who have very little knowledge about financial resources, thereby doing away with ignorance, which is precisely what the government does not want. Clever taxpaying people digging a way out from adverse circumstances.
In a broad sense as far as giving specific product recommendations individuals must carry out their own feasibility study like a treasure hunt to find what would best suit their practical needs, there are several ways of building a good income for the future, but the most sensible way is to have a pension, which in the long run becomes a steady income given to a person who has retired from active work, some retirement plan accumulate cash balance through a variety of mechanism known as superannuation. Some pensions are created by employers and they are for the benefit of their employees, it is a saving known as occupational pension, government may fund a part of these or the company may take on the full responsibility
But for more simplicity, financial planning could benefit a great deal by helping people with their budgeting and switching their debt to cheaper solution, however, I am not overly convince that people who fall into money mismanagement would bother using the financial advise line to get clear of bad debt, even if government made the information absolutely free.

Most would accept that society on a whole need to engage with people in work place, toughing up on employers to put on financial seminars that will benefit both company and employees. This pilot scheme is in operation in some innovative companies, but Sadly, if people's instinct is to go around and bury their head in the sand of ignorance, they will not be helping they until someone with extreme truth force them to face up to the harsh reality of life.

20. **Surviving a recession**

Recession is the state of the economy in decline, caused by economic negativity on domestic gross products, which is calculated over a period of two or more consecutive quarters, bringing a significant decline in economic activity which has wider implications; recession usually follows an increase of price in the oil industry until the economy peaks again.

Survival is not only a precedence for the fittest, it's a requirement in all aspect of life, especially where finance and job opportunities are concern, to survive we must know and have some indication of proof that recession is inevitable, having gather this information , it then alerts us to the possibility of forming a defensive options.

Governments that are blamed for allowing the country to fall into recession, have lots to answer for, when citizens are upset and are prepare to vent their anger in demonstration and withholding of support for political candidates, the long term solution will obviously have an effect on the national debt, which contributes at large to the economy.

To a wider degree, personal and business safe finances must always be protected, or greater damage will derived from the slowdown, complicating the

markets optimism, and as recession begins to bite, with the decline of productivity, the downturn will create more woes. But if categorized planning is in place, the effects of recession will only be minimal.
We should learn from past mistakes, that things are not going to get any better in the future, therefore all families should initiate of how to survive recession, unless we improve our personal economic circumstances, with profitable ideas, pulverizing our minds athleticism, while the cost of living is soaring higher and higher each day, early warning signs, suggest financial figures are approaching hazardous implications.
Verging on public corruption, people are resorting to survival horrors and secret nightmare activity bordering illegality, people are doing crazy things to stay on course in order pay their domestic bills, personal dept is climbing out of proportion, because the cost of living has raced out of control, and recession is approaching nervous imminence, and there will be a lot more money lost than is made, what you could have earned ten years ago for a week's wages, today it will only buy a handful of grocery.

Recession is two or more consecutive quarters of declining gross domestic products, and deep recession is at the risk of the economy going significantly

Past the quarter, and effecting unemployment, recession is a bigger threat to the economy than inflation, recession affects the running of business and has a sever knock on effect with individuals and families limiting the threat of recession must become the government's most urgent priority.

Recent movements in the financial sector, reveals a significant shift in the global market with gold dropping below $800 an ounce, as I had predicted before in my credit appraisal, also we see the continuing of the fall of oil. But for the long term future, we will face difficult days ahead, looking down from the barrel of a twin tunnel, we can clearly see a time of disruptive recession and inflation.

For a little while all will seemed good, backed up by a strong push of the dollar gaining ground against all other currencies, as sterling weakens against the strong dollar, the bank of England should cut interest rates before inflation reaches its peak. In many ways, planning to survive recession is similar to making preparation for one's own funeral, much care and thought will need to go into the planning.

What does inflation means to you? Inflation is prices running away above the governments suggested target, we must face up to recession with the rise in prices of goods, mainly oil and food products, where the cost is past unto the consumer, who will have to pay more for what they want, this effects major industrialize companies, by putting a strain on the labor output, when prices in the shops go up, people will complain that they can't afford to spend what they do not have.

Higher rate of Inflation is cause by the high rates growth of money supply, making inflation an overall rise on goods index, the long term trend can be difficult to predict because of the uncertain fluctuation, when things go up consumer spending tends to declined, widening the budget deficit and leaving public finances in a bad way, inflation rise concentrate on consumer spending, partly as a result of falling housing prices and commodities.

The commodity of yesterday's dreams is almost unidentified with the reality of the present consumer price index, today the money has turned to dust, declining in real value, when the Euro was at its peak the dollar was sagging, time is ripe for a transformation, the weak European economy may need a cut soon to cool inflationary pressures.

While the US economy has actually slowed down from turning into a decline, European interest rates twice has risen

Twice as high, the economy in Europe has weakened, offsetting the attraction to investors of European interest rates, it sends a gloomy picture of the economic outlook.

The bad news for longer term means construction may lay off workers, because the constructing of new homes has dropped off below the consistent pace, this could turn out good in housing favor stabilizing the market. But the credit crunch in Europe is not going to stop there, property, mortgages, pension's savings and unit trust, will all be affected.

Lively Imagination is going to be the amazing feat needed, to sustain the standard of living we have all been natured upon, The cries for help is coming from almost every householder, gas, electric and oil prices have doubled over the past few years, fuel cost has certainly put depleting limits on the family budget.

The prospect ahead is showing the government weakening grip on the economy, with annual consumer price inflation rocketing far above predicted targets, spending power has reduce the muscles of luxuries to an unpopular mirage, definitely nothing is working for the government, and hardly any savings has been put away, whenever one area is fixed, another area is festering lamely and needs a band aid.

There are dire consequences facing the global economy, because the house bubble has deflated, ominous signs are causing panic implications, the turn down has revive unemployment fears, each month increase has been greater than the previous unemployment figures, the numbers of people claiming job seekers allowance has risen in every month, and there are now more people receiving benefits than there were this time last year.

21. **Personal Finance: Preparing for a recession**

Usually recession doesn't happen too often, but when the forecast is imminent, the signs are apparent that the economy will go into distress mode, it's also a clear indication that personal finances will be severely affected, although the economy will suffer the brunt of difficulties, peoples jobs may be at risk, through layoffs and redundancies.

Preparation is needful to combat the long term effects that recession will have on individuals, as production output declines, trade and industry will find it hard to sustain credit facilities, they will have to figure out a way of saving money, the result will cause further shrinkage in available funds.

Preparation for recession is one of those essential necessity, it is sensible thinking to make allowance for emergencies, and crisis that will arise out of proportion, through no fault of our own, but by putting ourselves in an understanding position, the preparation that is made, will better qualify us to manage credit cards, make mortgage payments, settle school fees, and keep control of other domestic household responsibility.

Preparation should consist of cut backs in areas of wasteful spending, reducing some social activities, including expensive luxury holidays, make specific cut backs in the home entertainment center, unnecessary liability such as hiring movies, frivolous waste of money on dialing premium telephone numbers, making unsubstantiated large purchases, preparation consist of been more consistent in maintaining a working budget.

Most people like to spend money freely, but in recession that way of living can cost a lot of trouble, a budget is the best form of money management, it gives you an indication at a glance, to see where all your money is going, bear in mind, that once recession has arrived, it will take some time before it bottoms out, the financial preparation that is made for covering personal finances, will safe guard against the economy deteriorating further.

No one is certain about what will take place in the early months of recession, but if a person feels that their job will be under threat of redundancies or even been laid off for undisclosed periods of time, they should look around to secure extra employment, two or three part time position may be the answer to offset the negative possibility, these jobs will of course provide additional income to maintain the standard of living that a person has been accustom to.

Recession has deeper ramifications in causing global economic crisis, for America, Europe, and many other affluent countries, such as China, Japan, France, Germany, Finland, Ireland, and Italy. However, some commonwealth countries with their economy already crumbling beneath the weight of unpaid debt, are not only looking for humanitarian aids, but are looking for long term help to better prepare for the future, which could see neighboring countries swimming against the tide, with frightening dereliction of duty to their citizens.

And many poorer people, were already living in dreadful deficit of what appears to be normality, but retrospect, in recession, their condition will worsen to dire consequence, their only demand is necessity of getting food on a daily biases, so awful is there condition, it's hard to imagine how people survive, giving a million now and again, will result in a splash in the ocean of trouble, yet pitying them will not make their plight any better, but finding a solution to aid them in recovery will give back character some personal self esteem.

In hindsight, everyone hopes that conditions will improve, and the cost of goods will not increase, nor the raising of fuel consumption charges, but the important factor needs to be borne out, that without making preparation for how bills are going to be settle in the likely event of a recession, individuals along with businesses will struggle, putting a little aside in a separate account is positive thinking, cut down on unnecessary travel, will reduce the amount of outgoing expense, priorities what areas that are absolutely essential.

Making preparation to deal with recession will depending largely on your current financial state, if you have never invested in any form of savings, maybe now would be a good time to start putting some money into a worthwhile venture, with low risk investment if you are a cautious person.

If on the other hand, you are unsure how to go about investment, and making plans to cover emergencies, go see your bank manger or an investment broker, they will guide you into the area of gilt edge security, government bonds, stock s and shares, portfolio diversity, personal equity plan (PEP) private Pension, and a genuine idea of what a person can do to better themselves before it's too late.

People should learn how to regulate their personal finances in times of distress, and be smart with their money, by making it work for them in positive ventures and secure holdings, when consumer spending is bad, and trade and industry production has declined, individuals may have to dig deep into their reserve, to make payments on their homes and other essentials, if payments are not made on time, they risk defaulting on mortgages and loan agreement is high, which as we all know, can lead to foreclosure on most property.

At a later stage, possibly when recession has chalked up many causalities , government may step in with a stimulus package to nationalize some companies, by then it could have all been too late for many individuals, and especially those who had not made any kind of advance planning, they will feel the severe effects of recession.

What is credit crunch?

Credit crunch is the complete models of financial reckoning, severely affected, by the downturn of the US housing market where borrowers are allowed to borrow more than what the value of their assets were. Bankers will quickly agree that one of two inevitable things will happen, if your liability is greater than your assets.

You will go into negative equity, and difficulties will arise in repaying the loan, under normal circumstances, a person or company should not borrow more than what they can afford to pay back, tempting though the offer may be, a system of regulations is needed to stop all such overvalued loans been approved, it makes sense to know where the funds is coming from to make repayments.

Most people will borrow more than 3 times their annual salary on repayment mortgages, some go a lot higher, but that is where the danger signs are glowing brighter, the crunch comes when it's time to pay back, and there is not enough funds to make lodgments, because the risk has been vastly over miscalculated.

In tough times, equity plans and securities need to be revised, and there are no easy choices; Federal Reserve is not a financial fortress to bail out every eventuality created by mishaps crystallizing into greed. Injecting more cash into the toxic root of mortgage investment will encourage more bad decisions; unless we see some more shake down of banking neglects, bankers will continue to make a tidy sum of profit in the mud without accountability.

Banking was a very simple way of saving money and getting funding for a dream home, and for 158 years Leeman brothers did their money business, until greed began to take closer interest, now desperate moves are been made to avoid more causality of the credit crisis exposing their camouflage conflagration .

Mathematically, if a person has $1 to invest, and they invest it wisely, they will end up with $2 multiply that and you would still be a head of your initial capital investment, if somebody lends you another $1 and after you invest that you will have $4, after you have paid back $1 you would end up with $3 that's leverage.

Simple if you stay within the safety perimeters, but failure to invest correctly will result in sever reprimand, that is why the finest mind on Wall Street are combined to restructuring credit down grade, but they can find no confidence in the eroding industry, because none of the mathematics are adding up to wise business management.

The alternative was for the government to step in and bailed Lehman brothers out of the pit they had dug for themselves, choices would be to sell half or part of the share holding business, to raise the extra cash needed, the most hopeful plan was to split toxic mortgage investment away from the rest of the bank, but to no avail.

Here is how confidence in the banking industry was lost at the eleventh hour, Federal Reserve could not guarantee a blinking penny to sure up the gigantic liabilities, and for all their expertise, the bank was dead and the game was as good as lost.

Here is how the battle was lost, if you are an investor and you had $30bn to invest, through low interest rates, you persuade others to lend you one trillion, you will make a multi billion profit per year, but then you go further and pay out huge bonuses to the top earners, recycling all the money into loans for business to home buyers and small investors, that's leverage the wall street way, but the danger comes, when investments are taken out of context, forcing growth and going for larger profit margin resulting the misuse of investment is not managed properly.

The worse scenario is when investment ending up halving in value, and you are left with the initial $1 that you started with, but you also have to pay back the other $1 back to the lender, the outcome is that you will end up with nothing, if you should multiply that with wall street figures, you will see the real values of share prices wiped off leaving nothing but negative equity. When the pot is empty, the atmosphere becomes the doom of sinners, and the happiness of believers.

22. **Understanding inflation, and how it can affect your future**

The cost of living is soaring higher each day, figures newly out suggest cause for concern, adding more financial burden to the already hard pressed family budget, because the cost of living is alarmingly spiraling out of control, cries for help is coming from almost every corner of the world, the prospect ahead is showing a weakening grip on our national resources, annual consumer price inflation are hitting higher and higher percentages each month.

Abandoning the acquired wealthy status we had achieved with property development, and other lucrative investments during the past few years, we are now in real jeopardy of reverse negative equity. With pension performance not adding up to a whole heap, The disturbing downturn applies to the nation as well as to all individuals, at some stage most people will begin to feel the squeeze on their finances, and they will look to government for answers.

It means that inflation is running away above the governments suggested target, oil prices and food are the main violation which is causing the gloom to deepen, fuel products are far more expensive than a year ago, the economic climate is worrying with rising unemployment and spiraling personal debt, rising inflation is prompting fears that the economy is accelerating out of control.

As a result of these jittery anomalies, billions have been wiped of the stock market, plunging companies into uncharted territory and greater financial dilemma, mortgages and housing cost is also reacting to the atmosphere and the financial institutions are showing some unpleasant instability.

Inflation is the cost of consumer products, where prices are always on the increase over a period of time, so when inflation gets too high the cost of living is not sustainable, and some compromises have to be made, usually families on lower income feels the effect first, when inflation gets out of control, it reduces the value of our money, this influence affect the stock market.

Whenever the FTSE underperforms, the dramatic falls in share prices always have significant impact upon the investment of millions of families, while these families may have been inform by media about what is taking place, the government to a larger degree, bears the ultimate responsibility for creating the panic station of uncertainties.

However, most people don't trust what politician says, and even though they are trying to put a delicate spin on the matter, they should also be bracing themselves for more disappointing news in the future, a cut in interest rates is desperately needed, but the banks dare not do a thing like that, it will be hard to give us the interest rate cut we need to boost the economy, they will have the urge to do it, but not the will power to carry it out, when headline news on our financial data is not only alarming, but surprisingly high, much like the sinking of a great ship in icy waters, inflations deepens, and we are its victims.

So while the credit crunch is taking such a bruising toil upon all and sundries, it's fair to say, these actions are heightening the coming of a worldwide economic crisis. Where the latest dives have been blamed on the gloomy American economy, whenever Wall Street index tumbles, fears are made worsen, the fallout from us mortgages sends global shivers for more mounting assessment, and comparisons quickly leap to mind in quest for the right answers.

A dip in oil prices will readdress the equilibrium momentarily, and give investors a little bit more confidence, but beware, the trend is still upwards, and at the moment every piece of news is valuable, relief will only be short lived, and the flexing of greater mussels will soon be needed.

23. **Tips for credit card management**

Looking back on some important things that you need to know about Credit cards before you apply for one, first of all credit cards was first pioneered for the select few who had the means by which to pay back, steadily as their economy picked up, and they got more money, it gave customers a greater spending power, the rush for credit took on a new approach.

In recent years, credit cards have become more widely accepted in modern society, and it is a status symbol that is woven into our way of living, most people would feel absolutely insecure, when they are going shopping and travelling expedition, if they don't have their credit cards with them.

With the global economy moving closer into a recession of credit crunch, the atmosphere is changing the whole institutionalize way of thinking, and the opportunity is becoming more apparent, for financial backers to make their products more widely available for a new invigorated growing market. Creating an accessible payback solution. For those with good credit, while at the same time granting bad creditors the opportunity to repair their credit rating.

Credit cards is also available for individuals with less than perfect credit rating, however, good money management is a prerogative, which includes making payments on time above the minimum amount, having a credit card can help to improve a person's credit rating, if they maintain their obligation of financial consistency in repayments. There is definitely a minimum amount of payment that you must make each month, and this must be done to avoid higher interest charges.

Today's top credit cards, are the envy of most people, who are struggling on low income, good management is important to maintain payments, failure to pay your credit card bills on time, will obviously result in poor credit rating, and limit your prospect of getting any further credit from anywhere, to get good credit with a low APR, the prospect is limited to those with good credit history, but for the most part, this option is unavailable to consumers that have had a poor credit history, or no history at all.

While some individuals in the past had the misfortune of having bad credit, as a result of unemployment or illness, most consumers simply manage their finances badly. By not budgeting correctly, and cutting back on overspending, if you manage your credit card payments properly, You can apply for better facilities with lower APR, this will give you wider available spending power, and higher credit limit.
Credit cards management handled poorly, will keep credit rating low, and restrict your future prospect of obtaining credit facility.
We are quickly progressing to a cashless system of purchases. where consumer do not need to carry large sums of money around with them, to purchase necessities when they go shopping, however, by having a credit card it gives them the available means by which to pay. Credit cards give you the option to settle your hotel bill on check out.

Airline tickets, and car hire can also be paid for with a credit card, the possibilities is almost endless what you can do with your credit card. Credit in broad terms simple means cash when you need the resource, but how many credit cards do an individual need? That will largely depend upon the level of credit they want and can afford to utilize.

What are the benefits of having a credit card? Apart from the obvious, its available credit when you want, it can get you out of embarrassing situation, its character and status building. You can use your credit cards to pays bills; book holiday flights, pay for the weekly grocery shopping, and without leaving your armchair, you can fulfill your entire obligation on line. Credit cards can be used for identification purpose, as well as making all other necessary purchases.

A wise principle is to keep a small balance owing, which will give the credit company the opportunity to increase your balance, many financial experts will of course tell you, that it is to your advantage, that you should pay off your credit card balances as fast, and as quickly as possible, here is where you make the decision for good credit management.

Balance Transfers is what credit use to draw customers away to a different company with possibly a better APR. Companies will offer interest free for a disclosed period of time on your existing debt; they will do this in exchange for customers switching to their credit card.

This practice only benefits the credit card company, rather than improving individual status, because the more debt you incurred on credit cards, the less credit worthy you are likely to be. As a rule of safety, here is how to measure your credit, and stay one step ahead of the high charges, the answer is quite simply, to keep a little less than half, of your available credit limit open across all your credit accounts. That way it puts you in control of your finance.

Late fees are closely aligned with popular credit cards, this is a strong deterrent for customers to stay in line, and pay their bills on time, if they fail to make the minimum payment which is stated on their bill each month, then the over limit fees will apply, if you fail to stay, within your credit limit.

However, by keeping a small balance you will give the credit company the opportunity to increase your balance, many budgeting financial expert will of course tell you the plain advantage, that you should to pay off your credit card balances, as fast and as quickly as possible, in order to maintain good credit card management.

Chapter five

25. Should you keep all your money in one bank?

Depending on your personal circumstances, but the consensus is that you should not keep all your money in one back, because you will not allow your money to grow and give you back the right kind of returns. Banking at one branch may suit small business better, than for owners to have multiple accounts; many people have held the same account since they were fist year students.

Given the current state that banks are in as scapegoats goes, taking the brunt of the blame for the present financial crisis is greeted with applause in some sector of the industry, rather than letting people accept their own irresponsible behavior, saddled with toxic debts, banks have been handed a barrel of public cash by the government to rescue them from winding up in administration, it is obviously something of an escape route, made to relieve the huge blood pressure that they have been under.

The banking sector is competitive business which has opened a back door for government to manipulate, if they accept the bailout rescue stimulus on offer, the rescue plan will automatically inject the banks with fresh new capital which the government will provide to support loans for purchasing homes, maintaining businesses and stimulating the economy, the stimulus plan, brings the cost of the administration's economic rescue efforts to nearly $3 trillion.

Even with that massive handout to stabilize the nation's banking sector, the American public is still sceptical about government intervention to handle the crisis, and confidence is needed to restore faith in the banking industry, where a large percentage of people have their investment tied up in various saving accounts.

As if things weren't bad enough for high street banks with their huge debts and collective liquidity, banks have come under renewed attack, from customers are taking out their money and reinvesting with food chain stores, offering good deals on basic banking services such as savings on loans, expanded investment accounts and travelling insurance, with programs that provide overdraft protection on individual accounts. The need to keep your money in one bank depend upon your financial circumstances and what benefit can be derived from such actions.

Some may have been the unfortunate victim of credit card fraud, but have remained with the same bank, because of the overdraft facility that has provided flexible options.

Behind the smoke screened, millions of taxpayers cash has been committed to the banks rescue stimulus, on terms that often seems bewildering, in what appears to be a political unusual leap backwards into the dark ages, the exact magnitude of the unpleasantness surrounding banks is provoking anti banking feelings, right across the wide spectrum, some people are upset at the prospect of losing their homes, others have grave concern about bank managers who are walking away with large pots of gold in pension bonus.

Banking at one branch may suit small business better, than for owners to have multiple accounts; many people have held the same account since they were fist year students.

Sometimes when we hear of banks in trouble, and the news start to circulate, we see people aggressively queuing to take out their savings rather than depositing fresh amounts. This is an act of fearful uncertainty and the loss of confidence in that institutions, those who do not benefit from having their money in one bank, possibly have other sources of investment assets in material things

But every investor is looking for the best possible return on their money, so keeping all your money in one bank will largely depend upon several contributing factors, namely the suitability for personal lifestyle, and the aspect of social conveniences, but the primarily reason for keeping your money secure in one establishment, will undoubtedly be the type of service that a particular bank is offering its customer, along with all the charges and fees that are taken into consideration.

For many people, some charges that banks typically administered on accounts breaching contract, are deemed unfair and as a result, people feel oblige to make a complaint with threats of taking their business elsewhere, if you feel that at anytime you have been overcharged for services rendered by your bank, make an appointment to see the bank manager , and get these charges lifted or reduced, a mistake could possibly have accrued, If the fees are high there will be a tendency for account holders to be disenchanted with the service they have been given.

Interest rates are as low as they are ever likely to go, it's hardly worth keeping money in the bank, when there are other lucrative opportunities and different options, frequently popping up with smarter reductions in guaranteed income, the big switch could be cheaper for some, while costly for others, depending on the circumstances, but more rewarding benefits could derived from the proximity of the bank locally, the overall feeling would be for a person to keep the majority of their money in one bank, which may be good for providing checking facilities,

Depending on the level of business you will be putting towards the banks way, multiple choice in operating different types of account could prove more beneficial, by selecting another bank which is offering better interest on savings, the diversity could prove financially rewarding, first check that the charges you will be paying on your personal checking account will not be high.

The trend among some banks is to adopt a more stringent terms of holding conditions, limiting the total amount of withdrawal that can be made in one year, without painfully occurring additional cost.

Customers want instant access to their cash are looking for banks to provide long term relationship, by choosing the right savings account, which meet both banks and customer needs, customers are and not just looking for what appears to be the best rate appeal, although this is very important, and may be the very reason why you have chosen to place your money in that institution, it's always worth finding out beforehand what the company policies are with regards to withdrawal.

Personal wealth requires value and interest, so it is advisable to check the small prints before putting all your eggs in one basket, there may be some nasty hidden withdrawal penalties, with the potential to cause shock awaiting you around the corner, recovery may even take longer to clear up and profits certainly will be eaten up out of your savings.

26. Penalty for cash withdrawal

The trend among some banks is to adopt a more stringent terms of holding conditions, limiting the total amount of withdrawal that can be made in one year, without painfully occurring additional cost.

Customers want instant access to their cash are looking for banks to provide long term relationship, by choosing the right savings account, which meet both banks and customer needs, customers are and not just looking for what appears to be the best rate appeal, although this is very important, and may be the very reason why you have chosen to place your money in that institution, it's always worth finding out beforehand what the company policies are with regards to withdrawal.

Personal wealth requires value and interest, so it is advisable to check the small prints before putting all your eggs in one basket, there may be some nasty hidden withdrawal penalties, with the potential to cause shock awaiting you around the corner, recovery may even take longer to clear up and profits certainly will be eaten up out of your savings.

Instant access saving accounts have their place, and all are paying above the bank base rate, at present, with the increasing credit crunch, it is almost impossible for banks to raise the required cash they need, to bankroll mortgages and loans, cheap enough to attract interest buyers, the banks gladly wants your money, but they do not want to give back willingly when it comes down to withdrawal, unless there is something in it for them.

So in order to keep a hold of your money, and watch your interest dwindled, they have to pull in a litigious stranglehold on the resources of their ordinary savers, and they are then utilizing the power they have over existing savers, by keeping them camouflage in a longer relationship, the treatment is unfair, but shows willingness on the side of banks to execute negligence, if customers are inclined to break the agreement.

However, attracting new savers is good for the advertisement of the business, but in the long term, savers who are not counting the expenses will benefit the banks in greater measures. Making withdrawal too frequent shows one of possible tow things, first instant access accounts should be just that available at the drop of a hat, second that may not be that count that best suits your circumstances.

The trend among some banks is to adopt a more stringent terms of holding conditions, limiting the total amount of withdrawal that can be made in one year, without painfully occurring additional cost, consequently, the less amount of time you take money out of your account, banks will find themselves in a stronger position, by holding down tight on your money. With competition getting stiffer, the move is a contentious trust with winners in both categories.

The downside to this masquerade is in the best interest of the bank, if long term savers go over the limit of the amount of withdrawal in one year, there is a massive lost to the interest gained, the true term for these savings should really be instant access, but customers are not fully aware of these startling procedures, if they start exceeding the allowance woven in the contract, there will be a hefty price to pay.

Banks have cut the cost of you making too many trips to the withdrawal counter, by softening up the blow, and keeping the relationship going longer and cheap enough, they also lock your money into their own beneficial vault, but all these accounts lack transparency, and are been peddled to savers, as advisable best form of accounts, for me the best form of accounts is not paying out a penalty, but gaining a large bonus that will not easily disappear.

Overview

Banks exist to serve individual consumers, with useful financial products; the market is largely attracted to business customers from all different kinds of levels, seeking personal and convenient banking requirements.

The bank of America remains one of the world's largest financial institutions, with view of expanding more of their financial products to meet individual needs. The bank focus on making money, that is their first priority, they also exist, to provide a full array of loan facilities, such as mortgages, pensions, investments, personal loans, bridging loans and savings accounts.

Today, the banks in the US has expanded significantly, serving businesses and communities with their powerful financial sector, safeguarding a reputable legacy dating back to the early 1980s, when banks played an integrated part in the lives of students and new home owners.

There is a level of unprecedented vibrancy with the innovated example of sponsorship invent Banks provide the financial solution for acquisition of stadiums, and players, as market leaders the focus on opportunities with minimalist risk.

Banks are the capitalist for control in all major sporting events, and the flexible support bank rolling sports has given the victory to produce more revenue assets.

The overall performance of the banks rely largely on customers, healthy profit reflects valuable premium for shareholders.

Control transaction offers individuals and business the security of investment, with their team of financial advisers they will seek to invest the manage funds in stocks and shares, where they will get a good return for deposits invested.

US Banks provide the financial solution for acquisition of stadiums, player's wages, agency fees, as market leaders the focus on opportunities with minimalist risk.

Banks in the us will help fans to connect to their individual sports, by allowing them overdraft facilities, and easy access to money, in the critical economic times banks continues to play a pivotal role in providing financial resources for business to continue trading, their objective is to make the impact of positive feedback a substantial ground for a better living.

US banks have in place the capital structure for controlling monetary transactions. Bringing together individuals, communities, and businesses in time, they will unveil him full range of financial products can help companies to expand and franchise.

A team of financial advisors provides advice over the phone, based on a holistic view of your financial situation
Get a personalized strategy to help you pursue your financial goals
Receive investment recommendations with a foundation in mutual funds, as well as a mix of investments suited to your needs
Receive two written portfolio reports a year and ongoing access to advice when you need it
Track changes in your portfolio with free, automated account monitoring, pay close attention to all money talk in your life, it's the life blood flowing to nearly all areas of our lives, sometimes with healing, at other times, money can become a god, and therefore an unnecessary burden. But no one will give it to you free, all must work for it.

Generally for clients with more complex financial needs, especially those who want to work with a dedicated financial advisor and want to invest $250k or more through different financial agencies will see their personal financial gamble pay off.

Build a relationship with a Financial Advisor who will work with you to create a holistic strategy that can help you meet your goals -- from retirement to investments to estate planning
Know your Financial Advisor has the support of product specialists to help recommend appropriate solutions
Receive advice and guidance to help you keep your investments aligned with your long term strategies for your personal finances.

The best value vacation for your money

There is an epigraph in meticulously choosing between the overspend vacation, and the narrow conceptual idea of bridging the gap of affordability , vacation brought by glamour and happy snappy commercials, where sales techniques lavishly attracts the attention unearthing all our hard earn finances, and putting romantic feelings into deluded promises of fulfilling exotic dream holidays,

Many of those highly rated holiday adverts are not worth the price they are asking, however, to sensibly cut the cost of rising vacation cost, there is an economical way that could benefit most people, the solution is simply to take that vacation and stay at home, and it's the best value for your money.

The advantages is that you will receive lots more benefits, by staying at home you can cut the cost of a vacation and still get the desired rest and relaxation that the body cries out for, you may not get to go to all the places that you would dream of going to, but you can enjoying nearer home, because your locality is also a fabulous place for gleaming knowledge, by sharing some of the well chosen amenities that are available, you can enjoy the swanky luxury of your own home without time constraint.

Because of the credit crunch associated with our financial limitations, the interaction is perfectly encapsulating, and current atmosphere brings the opportunity to finely balance family budget, the credit crunch that is affecting everyone at the moment, need not be a complete disaster, and apart from those profiteering millionaires.

Who may not be feeling the squeeze, most families have to carefully plan their budget for any meaningful vacation they want to take, and they have to do this with careful distinct touches. Sometimes ruthlessly cutting corners and ending up with less than the barging that they had hoped for, some barging comes in disguise of horror hotel service, lifeless resorts and ample pick pockets.

Many people will find themselves in the position where they have the time off work but have very little funds to utilize the time with, vacation days can be a great way of discovering the community in which you live, by visiting the local parks with beautiful gardens you can acquire valuable local knowledge, lots of people who live in their community do not know where the parks and recreation centers are found, they remain in ignorance at the vast wealth of opportunity that has been invested into their own locality, and insisted in paying absurd and extortionate prices for something that they can easily get for nothing on their own door steps.

Having travel to the west indies, Africa, Europe, America, and other under privileged parts of the world, I am amaze at how comfortable people have made their simple existence a place of contented retreat, just because a person pays thousands of dollars to go on Safari to see the fabulous animal kingdom, it does not make that holiday any better than the person who stays at home and enjoy the changing seasons and familiar privileges.

The locals you see when you go on Safari lives daily within their own environment and see those animals every day breathing the same air, a safari guide very rarely goes on any distant holiday, they take into consideration that affordability is a dilemma, disruption of routine, fear of the unknown, they take their vacation at home, and home can consist of just bare necessities to get by, take a look how happy they are with how little they possess.

And yet people travel thousands of miles to experience what they have within their grasp, they make use of local knowledge, having the wisdom and understanding to know when and where to shelter from the harsh terrain, been razor Sharpe in sensing danger, aggressive with security, using plant life for medical purposes, rivers and trees, the moon and stars all plays a part in their natural habitation, something that no amount of expense can afford.

Make use of your days off work, carefully plan your budget to stay at home and enjoy the Botanical gardens that are within walking distance, wear holiday slacks to keep you in the mood, make your time interesting and innovating, nearby parks and botanical gardens are filled with bright colors and they exhibit a lively environment in which nature comes alive to build your vast reservoir of enviable knowledge.

There are so many botanical gardens and glasshouses where you can enjoy nature at its best and discover the importance of plants and how they interact with people's lives. Passion bears fruit, and you may find yourself waking up with the passion of knowledge that most people can only marvel at.

If you have time off from work, but you do not have any surplus money in your budget to go that step further anywhere exotic. Then be realistic, take a stay at home vacation, home is where the heart is, marinate your taste appetite with a course in home cocking, this may be a way of spicing up your life, because it's absolutely crazy eating food you don't want to eat, the result is always the same, diarrhea and sickness, experience by tourist in hot countries.

You certainly do not have to feel disappointed if you cannot afford an expensive holiday, there are lots of enjoyment to look forward to at home, and plenty to do, theater to attend, movies to catch up on, books and magazine to read, without laboring the point, you can do so much more with your time passionately and progressively that will give you a possible greater geographical satisfaction than a dangerous trip to the back waters of some uncivilized country, governed by desperate despots, vaguely aware of the Internet global conquest.

Of course there are some advantages and disadvantages of staying at home, you will gain interactive entertainment with the family, and there is no rush to check in on time for a flight, no large bags to pack or passports to be updated, the search for gifts and deciding what duty free item to choose, evening and morning can be triumphant collaborated with extraordinary moments of repose and sleep.

I must point out that you also will use less energy than you would in snorkeling or taking part in banana adventurous rides, where you are scared witless from some dare devil meandering wind tunnel, caught between the climax pleasure of touching humanity and the realism of been dragged off to an early heaven.

First there are no great demand on your time schedule, no large cash outlay or worried about mosquito and insect repellents, or acquiring visa, it could be financially rewarding and the assurance to know that you will not be going into more negative Debt just for the sake of visiting an exotic country, most people will come back to face a hefty credit card bill if you could not afford the vacation in the first place.

Use the money that your premiums has made to treat yourself to an exotic holiday, money just lying around in the bank cannot help you long after you leave this life, so enjoy the pleasure of its company while it last. Our days are as the wind, and soon the afternoon of twilight will descend, and all our savings others will inherit.

Be wise, utilizing the calm assurance that you can relax in the privacy of your own time and go out at your own leisure, remember that some far away destinations can leave you jaded, feeling more exhausted and disappointed than before you went away, dealing with the jet lag is also a problem that has to be overcome, and you would still need to take another break when you arrive home, maybe you will have to go to the Lake District or spend a few days just lounging about to unravel the pressure, So for a low budget holiday it's a good idea, with sensible cost effective plan, to enjoy a vacation at home.

This way the whole family can enjoy this treat, sometimes it could be worth your while just to take a home vacation by yourself. It is simply a great way of catching up on things at home in your own leisure, and the plus is that you can still do the normal day to day things, like taking the dog for a walk, go for a long run and recover in time for diner, and even do some shopping followed by some moderate household chores.

Important rules to follow

Discuss finance together in marriage, before proposal and during the married period open a joint checking account that will be used to pay the household bills, But for flexibility and access, it's a good policy to have separate bank accounts, be independent, and have your own personal bank account. Make regular lodgment into several investment accounts

For some people the word Budget because they like to spend what they do not have, and pay later, let me tell you this is a dangerous ploy. And before long you will end up in a lot of debt.

Budget

Always work by a budget, this is the new yes for the future

Provide receipts and give accurate account of money used for groceries, gas, rent, mortgage, utilities, clothes, tuition, vacation money, list emergency money and itemize all potential medical expenses that may arise in the future, know exactly where you are with your finances,

Accurate Accounts

Keep an accurate record of all income and expenditure

List both of your monthly expenses on a separate sheet of paper.

Pay close attention to small detail, every penny counts,

Name that game

Don't play games with your money, you could lose the lot.

Use your credit cards for important household expenses; your credit card is not Santa Clause

Spouse or partner should have their own credit card so they can establish a good line of credit.

When discussing your finances, get someone who knows what they are talking about.

Handle money with care, or someone else will take from you without a care in the world.

Proof

6655297R0

Made in the USA
Charleston, SC
18 November 2010